SUSTAINABLE SUSHI

SUSTAINABLE

Sushi

A Guide to Saving the Oceans
One Bite at a Time

Casson Trenor

North Atlantic Books
Berkeley, California

Published by

North Atlantic Books
P.O. Box 12327
Berkeley, California 94712

Cover photograph by Kristen Policy
Cover and book design by Claudia Smelser
Illustrations by Katie Burgess and Ben Smith
Art on disposable sushi containers by Alicia Escott

Printed in Singapore

Sustainable Sushi: A Guide to Saving the Oceans One Bite at a Time is sponsored by the Society for the Study of Native Arts and Sciences, a nonprofit educational corporation whose goals are to develop an educational and cross-cultural perspective linking various scientific, social, and artistic fields; to nurture a holistic view of arts, sciences, humanities, and healing; and to publish and distribute literature on the relationship of mind, body, and nature.

North Atlantic Books' publications are available through most bookstores. For further information, call 800-733-3000 or visit our website at www.northatlanticbooks.com.

LIBRARY OF CONGRESS CATALOGING-IN-PUBLICATION DATA

Trenor, Casson.
    Sustainable sushi / Casson Trenor.
        p.   cm.
    Includes index.
    ISBN 978-1-55643-769-4
    1. Cookery (Fish)   2. Sushi.   3. Sustainable fisheries.
I. Title.
    TX747.T655 2009
    641.3'92-dc22

                                        2008038260

1 2 3 4 5 6 7 8 9   TWP   14 13 12 11 10 09 08

This book is dedicated to the friends and family of Rusty Mowat, and to the memory of Tsuneko Okawara. Your blessing meant the world to me. I wish we could have met, if even just once. Rest well, *obaasan*.

TABLE OF CONTENTS

ACKNOWLEDGMENTS

First and foremost, my deepest gratitude to George Leonard, Jesse Marsh, and Corey Peet: your fierce commitment to protecting our oceans is what made this book possible. Thank you so very much.

To Pete Heller: a great writer is set apart not by what they themselves do, but by what they inspire in others. This book is as much yours as it is mine.

To Kin Wai Liu and Raymond Ho: eco-warriors of the highest order. Your bravery, honor, and determination are unparalleled.

To Katie Burgess, Alicia Escott, Tim Fitzgerald, Shana Hinds, Kristen Policy, Ben Smith, and Luis Velez: each of you graced this project with your unique gifts and talents. It would be so much less than it is without you. Thank you.

To my editor, Elizabeth Kennedy, whose patience is as vast and unending as the Pacific Ocean: thank you for your tolerance of all those things that can make working with me so intolerable.

To my esteemed colleagues at the Conservation Alliance for Seafood Solutions: I am constantly humbled and inspired by your dedication to our planet. Thank you for all that you do, and for all that you have taught me.

Although he himself would never set foot inside a sushi restaurant, I owe a great deal to my friend Paul Watson, who taught me about perseverance and integrity in trying times. Deep in the Antarctic ice, he unknowingly helped me to form the foundation of this book.

And, of course, none of this would have happened without the unyielding support of my mother, father, and sister. My love to you all.

And all you other wonderful people, in no particular order:

Dave "Davina Dobcaraz" Dobrowski
Nina "Davina Dobcaraz" Alcaraz
Bridget McDave
Don Rothaus
Brent Vadopalas
Cheryl Sindell
Elana Silver
Evelyn Rivera

Dennis Marks
Deanne Herman
Stacy Duke
Ron Colby
Monica Way
Hallie Gardner
Emily Brown
Nick "The Majestic" Tomb
Mike Hamilburg
Hannah "Wynne Hillegass" Hogan
Markus Naerheim
Jason "Joie Krak" Calsyn
Janet Sollod
Renee Mungas
Anya Shapina
David Lee
Jason Scorse
Laura Viggiano
Winifred Hui
Tobias Aguirre
Lisa Monzón
Susan Bumps
Nicole Andris
Harrison "Flip" Bains
Toby Barlow
Allegra Harris
Danny Glover
Talia Shapiro
Stephanie Danner
The Staff of Tataki Sushi and Sake Bar
The LBs of DR

Illustrations by Katie Burgess and Ben Smith.

Cover and book design by Claudia Smelser.

Photography by Kristen Policy.

Oil and inks on disposable plastic sushi containers by Alicia Escott.

Food styling by Raymond Ho and Kin Wai Liu.

Copy editing by Shana Hinds of the Northwest Independent Editors Guild and Christopher Church.

INTRODUCTION

love sushi. Really, I do. It's my favorite cuisine, and it has been since I tried it for the first time on my ninth birthday. I was enraptured by the feel, texture, and overall exotic nature of the ultrafresh fish and succulent sticky rice, and I've been hooked ever since. It became a celebratory staple—birthday dinners, parties, dates; any event would do. Sometimes I'd invent reasons to celebrate just to go nibble on *sashimi* at my local hangout.

It's precisely because of this long-standing love affair that a large part of me did not want to write this book. I've studied the demise of numerous fisheries and know the warning signs: destructive fishing practices, lack of management and enforcement protocols, questionable stock estimates. Many of the fish we see at the sushi bar are suffering from such problems, and I knew what this book would look like: I knew what research into the U.S. sushi industry would show. So many of my favorite dishes—mouthwatering *toro,* silky *ankimo,* sultry *unagi*—were not going to look good from a conservation perspective. But ignoring a problem doesn't make it go away. So I did the research. I studied the scientific findings. And I wrote this book.

The Japanese have a saying—*itadakimasu*—which literally translates as, "I take your life." While today it is a polite thing to say before any meal, the phrase is rooted in an acknowledgement that often, one creature dies for another's survival. Maintaining an awareness of this maxim is imperative for the responsible consumer. In this era of large-scale factory farming and prepackaged goods, it is precisely this connection, this knowledge of the bond between all living things, that we have lost. When we eat sushi, we usually eat fish—fish that were once living, breathing animals—and we do indeed take their lives. This is not a bad thing, per se, but it is perhaps more significant than we often realize. After all, our choices have consequences. That fish could have lived, bred, and given life to a new generation. It might have even become food for another species of fish, thereby contributing to the health of the marine food chain. Instead, it was caught and sold to a sushi restaurant for human consumption.

Now, before going any further, let me ease your fears: I am not going to tell you to stop eating fish. The goal of this book is not to tear you away from your favorite sushi bar. I don't want to forbid you the joys of fresh *nigiri,* nor the exhilaration of that extra smidgeon of *wasabi* on your tongue; just the opposite, in fact. If, as a society, we are aware of the consequences of our seafood choices, we can continue to eat sushi and protect our oceans at the same time. Moreover, we will better understand how our choices may affect our health, positively or negatively.

This book is a reference tool covering about forty of the fish and shellfish (listed both by their English and in Japanese names) most commonly found at a North American sushi bar.It will provide an overview of where and how a fish is caught, what kind of shape the populations are in, whether or not the fish may contain pollutants, and other important facts. Each fish also receives a basic recommendation—generally either "enjoy" (green), "use caution" (yellow), or "avoid" (red). From this baseline, you can start to construct your own personal plan for sustainable dining without turning your back on the sushi counter. Switch bluefin out for albacore, order wild salmon instead of farmed, try *mirugai* instead of *hokkegai*. You'll be surprised at how easy it can be to change an ordinary sushi dinner into a sustainable one.

Sustainable Sushi: A Guide to Saving the Oceans One Bite at a Time can help us find a better way to appreciate this unique cuisine. If we are aware of the long-term effects of our seafood choices, we can ensure the survival of the ocean and its bounty—as well as the art of sushi itself—for many years to come.

See you at the sushi bar.

Itadakimasu!

WHAT IS SUSTAINABILITY?

The concept of sustainability has been bandied about so much that one could see it as almost meaningless. Formally introduced in 1987, it has over the last two decades taken on any number of meanings, many of which are competing and contradictory. It is sometimes said that in a room of 10 people there are 10 different definitions of sustainability.

The word is applied in any number of situations, some appropriate and some otherwise. It's used by companies to sell products and by environmentalists to boycott the same products. It has become a buzzword, a nonsense term. So maybe it's best to go back to the basics and start at the beginning.

Sustainability, according to *Webster's Dictionary:*

> a: of, relating to, or being a method of harvesting or using a resource so that the resource is not depleted or permanently damaged (*sustainable* techniques) (**sustainable** agriculture) b: of or relating to a lifestyle involving the use of sustainable methods (*sustainable* society)

As the formal definition states, sustainability is about stewarding resources in such a way that they are available in the future. At face value this is fairly straightforward.

However, once we apply sustainability more broadly to include environmental, economic, and social components it becomes trickier to define. Many environmentalists claim that for a resource to truly be managed sustainably, it must be utilized in a way that takes all three of these concepts into account.

Environmental sustainability is the main focus of this book. In terms of seafood, concerns over environmental sustainability prompt questions such as: How was this fish caught or raised? Is it intrinsically a vulnerable species, due to a long natural life, low reproductive capability, slow maturation rate, or other characteristics? Are we overfishing the stock? Does a given fish farm pollute or have adverse effects on the environment? Does the manner in which we are catching a particular fish harm other species? Does a given fishery negatively impact the earth or the oceans, or our future ability to catch this fish?

Economic sustainability has to do with making resource exploitation feasible for industry and providing sufficient employment. To follow with the fishing example, one might ask: Does this fish reproduce quickly enough to form the basis for a solid industry? Is the industry taking climatic and oceanographic trends into account? Is the fish so valuable that we may over-exploit it?

Social sustainability is about the people involved in the trade, as well as their history and culture. Sometimes we want to steer clear of environmentally unsustainable resources, but what does that mean for the people involved? Questions might include: If we stop all fishing in this area, how will the local fishermen survive? Are these fishermen able to sell their product for enough to provide for their families?

It is extremely difficult to consider all of these dimensions without a deep understanding of all aspects of a resource, the industry that exploits it, and the people that make up that industry. *Sustainable Sushi* is not an attempt to do so. Rather, this book concentrates on the environmental dimensions of the sushi industry. I acknowledge that this does not address all the components of sustainability, but I feel that it is an important and appropriate place to start.

We live in a society that is only now beginning to take the concept of sustainability seriously. Learning to live with it in mind will not be easy, and we must work together ... but we must start now, regardless of the discomfort, if we are to save the last vestiges of our once-great fisheries.

Remember as well that the status of the world's fisheries is dynamic, as is our understanding of them. The information in this book is current as of the time of writing but is subject to change with new information and science. To dine in as informed a manner as possible, check www.sustainablesushi.net for updates.

On this tiny planet of ours, sustainability is the future. Today the sushi bar, tomorrow the world.

MERCURY, FISH, AND YOUR HEALTH

Fish is supposed to be good for you. For decades, fish has been advertised as brain food: essential for child development and good for your memory. Its omega-3 oils also contribute to cardiovascular health. Over the last century, however, industrial pollution from power plants, waste incinerators, and mining operations have contributed to a pronounced increase in our oceans' mercury levels. This mercury, not surprisingly, is in turn gobbled up by the animals that call these waters home.

Sea life accumulates mercury mainly by consuming contaminated food. In areas near runoff sites, bottom-dwelling animals often have high mercury levels; these "detritivores" generally eat whatever they find on the seabed around them, much of which may be contaminated. In the open ocean, the highest mercury levels are usually found in the long-lived fish and predators that eat at the top of the food chain.

A debate rages over whether or not the mercury levels in fish have an impact on human health, and if so, whether or not the benefits of eating fish are outweighed by the mercury risks. Researchers have demonstrated links between contaminated fish consumption and numerous health issues, including developmental delays in children, increased cardiovascular risk, and decline in motor and brain function. In the United States the Environmental Protection Agency (EPA) has defined a "reference dose," which describes the amounts of mercury that can be safely ingested without appreciable health risks. While some dismiss the reference dose as unnecessarily cautious, many others, among them notable scientists and environmentalists, criticize it for not being stringent enough.

Bluefin tuna, king mackerel, shark, marlin, and swordfish are some of the species that accumulate the highest levels of mercury. They eat voraciously and may live for many years. In fact, these fish often contain many times more mercury than what is considered to be safe by the EPA.

Many experts claim that mercury is more dangerous for young and unborn children than it is for the average adult. This is due to the characteristics of the human blood-brain barrier, a semipermeable membrane that controls the flow of blood and nutrients between the bloodstream and the brain. In a fetus or young child, this barrier is more easily penetrated by mercury, which is then able to affect the entire brain. This process is inhibited in adults by a more developed and restrictive blood-brain barrier. Mercury is also concentrated in umbilical cord blood, further increasing exposure for unborn children.

Sustainable Sushi aims to give the average sushi diner accurate and honest information about the likelihood of high mercury levels in various marine animals. This information is presented for many fish to help sushi patrons make their own informed decisions about the benefits and risks of eating fish.

The mercury notifications in *Sustainable Sushi* assume a three-ounce portion of fish (about four pieces of *nigiri* or one good serving of *sashimi*). Rankings are based on scientific data compiled by the Environmental Defense Fund (EDF)[1] and the Environmental Protection Agency's Guidance for Assessing Chemical Contaminant Data for Use in Fish Advisories.[2] Mercury recommendations correspond to the number of servings that an average adult (weighing 154 pounds) can safely eat per month and are structured as follows:

MERCURY RISK	SAFE LEVEL OF CONSUMPTION (per month)
Low	More than 10 servings
Moderate	6–10 servings
High	3–6 servings
Extreme	Less than 3 servings

Other toxins are present in our seafood as well. Some of the most egregious offenders are polychlorinated biphenyls, or simply PCBs. PCBs were used in a number of industrial applications, such as for coolants and stabilizers in various electronic components and devices. Their production was banned in the United States in the 1970s due to health concerns, but they still persist in the environment to this day. PCBs are classified as "persistent organic pollutants"—carbon-based industrial problem children that, due to their chemical stability, take many years to break down. Numerous U.S. rivers and harbors have served as dumping grounds for PCBs, where they are consumed by local aquatic life (and potentially humans). PCBs have been linked to severe skin irritation, menstrual disruption, decreased immune function, liver damage, and cancer.

Throughout this book, all fish containing significant levels of PCBs will display a warning stamp: (PCB)

PREPARING YOURSELF
FOR SUSTAINABLE DINING

Let's face it—converting to a sustainable lifestyle isn't easy. Our cultural standards of behavior are often based on unsustainable

1. See www.edf.org/page.cfm?tagID=17694
2. See www.epa.gov/waterscience/fish/guidance.html

models. To make the shift to a sustainable way of life, we first have to cultivate an awareness of how our everyday choices affect the environment. This book is designed to help with that by focusing on the tiny little part of our lives that revolves around sushi.

Old habits die hard, and favorite foods are difficult to renounce. Sure, we might know what the "correct" choice is, but how realistic is it to say that we simply won't eat unsustainable options anymore? Or that we will ask our waitperson question after question about species, countries of origin, and catch methods?

Here are five tips that can help ease the transition to a sustainable sushi experience.

- *Take your time.* Work up to it. You can't be expected to change deep-rooted habits in one night. Make the necessary changes over a few visits rather than all at once.

- *Be inquisitive, yet friendly.* You may have to ask a lot of questions. Keep an open mind and a smile on your face; this will help to get you the answers you need.

- *Sit at the bar.* The chef is the one who knows the most about the fish being offered. If you don't have to send your waitperson back to the chef every time, asking questions doesn't feel like such an imposition.

- *Stick to your principles.* Sometimes it is hard—but remember, that *toro* really did come from the belly of an endangered bluefin tuna. That *ankimo* really is the liver of a monkfish. Be strong. Trust me, the mackerel, farmed abalone, and other options provided in this book are delicious as well as sustainable.

- *Tell your friends.* Get your family and dining partners on the sustainability wagon. If the whole party is committed to eating in a responsible manner, it becomes much easier to hold to your ideals.

There are lots of reasons that one might order questionable items. Perhaps the chef has a delicious, but notoriously unsustainable, special that he desperately wants you to try. Maybe your server is extremely busy, and you feel bad asking constant questions about catch methods and species particulars. These situations are understandable, and they do happen. Remember, just by reading this book, you're participating in a movement that is still in its infancy—a movement toward a more responsible way of eating.

So pace yourself. Make the transition over the course of a few visits. Some people are daunted by the enormity of the task, and they give up entirely. That's why we all need to remember that every little bit helps. Remember, it's not just about giving things up; it's about recognizing the importance of foods that we often take for granted.

So thank you for taking the steps you've already taken. Thank you for reading this book, and for giving sustainable dining a chance. Now, go put it into practice. Order sustainably. Eat well. Have a wonderful meal.

COLOR KEY

SUSTAINABLE: These fish and shellfish are caught or farmed in ways that don't have any major adverse effect on the environment. Strong stocks, insightful management, and low by-catch protect wild fisheries, while sustainable farms have little or no impact on their surrounding environment and demand little from our oceanic resources.

USE CAUTION: Animals in this category are from fisheries that are either poorly understood or have some troubling characteristics. While consuming them is probably not as destructive as eating fully unsustainable options, it is best to limit your consumption of these animals.

UNSUSTAINABLE: fish and shellfish are caught or farmed in a manner that is inordinately deleterious to the health of the oceans. These animals should be avoided until we overcome the particular challenges that they present.

SUSTAINABLE SUSHI

ABALONE / AWABI

Haliotis spp.

Abalone can be one of the best or one of the worst options at the sushi bar. The key issue is whether the animal in question has been farm-raised or illegally poached.

Abalone has been considered a desirable delicacy in the United States for years and as a result has suffered severe population declines. In certain areas, such as the California coast, steps are being taken to preserve those few animals that remain. Unfortunately, poaching is still a problem; there is good money to be made by selling illegal abalone to chefs and restaurateurs of dubious integrity.

For the conscientious sushi consumer, there are two main advantages to farmed abalone. The first and more obvious is that farming abalone lessens the pressure on wild populations. The second benefit springs from the abalone's herbivorous diet. Unlike some other farmed seafood (such as shrimp), abalone do not consume detritus or other animals; they subsist entirely on algae. Marine farms often generate significant pressure on wild fish populations due to their need for a constant supply of protein; abalone farms do not create this problem.

AWABI / ABALONE

It is important to discern what species of abalone is being served. Certain species are farmed, and are therefore more sustainable, while others are almost certainly wild-caught. In the United States, the red abalone (*Haliotis rufescens*) is the most prevalent species in marine farming, while wild abalone harvesters may take black, green, or pinto as well as wild red. In Asia the small abalone (*H. diversicolor supertexta*) and disc abalone (*H. discus hannai*) are the main farmed species.

Farmed abalone is generally about four inches across when harvested. If a larger specimen is found in a U.S. sushi restaurant, it could have been poached, especially if it is not red abalone. In such a situation, it may be prudent to question the chef about his or her sources.

Farmed abalone is a delicious alternative to less sustainable options such as giant clam, shrimp, and other rich shellfish. Wild abalone, however, should be consumed only rarely, and even then with great care and inquiry.

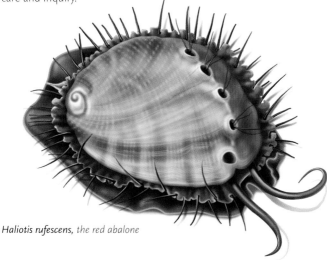

Haliotis rufescens, the red abalone

SOURCE
Farmed
Wild
Mercury risk: Low

3

ALBACORE TUNA / *SHIROMAGURO*

Thunnus alalunga

The menu term *shiromaguro*, literally "white tuna," refers to the roses-and-cream flesh of the albacore. Albacore tuna has long been a staple item in the United States, available at grocery stores across the country. When canned, albacore is labeled "chunk white" or "solid white" tuna. The technical Japanese term for albacore is *binnagamaguro*.

In the United States, the popularity of tuna sushi and *sashimi* continues to skyrocket. As can be expected, this increase in demand has placed additional pressure on tuna stocks, many of which were already in poor shape. Luckily, the albacore has certain attributes that make it a better choice than other tuna.

Albacore tuna mature quickly and breed rapidly. This makes them resilient to heavy fishing—but not immune. Some albacore populations are already weak, especially those in the North Atlantic and Indian oceans. Extreme pressure can devastate any fishery, so caution must be encouraged.

The major issue with albacore is bycatch. Bycatch occurs when fishing gear catches an animal other than the one it is targeting. Fish caught as bycatch are often worth less than the targeted fish, so rather than waste the ship's storage space, the bycatch fish—already dead—are dumped over the side. To make matters worse, bycatch isn't limited to fish—tuna longlines are known to ensnare and kill seabirds, sea turtles, and other unsuspecting animals.

Bycatch is a terrible problem with tuna fisheries that use longlines. It is very difficult to regulate what fish are attracted to the longline hooks,

SHIROMAGURO / ALBACORE TUNA

so bycatch is very high in many longline fisheries. The only obvious exception to this is in Hawaii, where the albacore longline fishery is particularly well-managed.

It is best to eat albacore that is troll- or pole-caught, as these methods use a pole with a single hook. This is a much easier system to regulate, and fishing this way greatly reduces bycatch.

Here's a breakdown of the most common albacore options:

Pacific troll-caught albacore from the contiguous United States, Hawaii, or Canada is one of the best ways to enjoy tuna at the sushi bar. With relatively strong stocks and a low bycatch rate, *shiromaguro* from these fisheries is an excellent choice.

Longline albacore from Hawaii and the North Pacific (U.S. and Canada) is a decent alternative. It has less bycatch and better management than other longline albacore fisheries, but it is still not an optimal choice.

U.S. Atlantic and imported troll-caught albacore is a somewhat satisfactory option. Bycatch is relatively low in these fisheries, but stock status and management effectiveness vary widely.

All longline albacore, with the exception of the Hawaiian option discussed above, should be avoided. Many international albacore fisheries are largely unregulated, with highly disturbing levels of bycatch.

SOURCE	CATCH METHOD	
U.S. Pacific and Hawaii	**Troll-caught**	Longlined
Canada Pacific	**Troll-caught**	Longlined
U.S. Atlantic	Troll-caught	**Longlined**
Imported	Troll-caught	**Longlined**

Mercury risk: Moderate

AMBERJACK / HAMACHI, ETC.

Seriola spp.

The rich buttery flavor and smooth texture of amberjack has achieved real popularity with American sushi fans. Be warned, however—to get to the bottom of the *hamachi* question, one must first establish what exactly is being served. That is not easy. First off, there are four species of amberjack that are found at the sushi bar. To make matters worse, mistranslations are extremely common: *Hamachi* isn't actually "yellowtail" at all. And the final monkey wrench: Names can change depending on age, size, and location.

So, let's start at the beginning.

The most common of the four species of amberjack used in sushi is *Seriola quinqueradiata,* the Japanese amberjack. It is properly translated as *hamachi*, although age and location can affect the name used. Hamachi is not yellowtail, regardless of what most menus claim; that title properly belongs to its close relative, S. lalandi, the yellowtail amberjack. This fish is known as *hiramasa* in Japanese.

S. dumerili, the greater amberjack, is also found in sushi restaurants from time to time, and is translated as kanpachi. Also, new farming techniques have resulted in an influx of S. *rivoliana*, the almaco jack, which is technically known as *hirenaga-kanpachi* in Japanese.

Simple, elegant, and unsustainable: **hamachi nigiri**

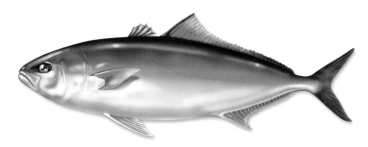

The Japanese amberjack, before it was your negihama roll

Here's a chart translating the most common terms for amberjack:

JAPANESE NAME	LOCALE	SCIENTIFIC NAME	ENGLISH NAME
Buri*	All Japan	*Seriola quinqueradiata*	Japanese amberjack
Hamachi†	Kansai region	*Seriola quinqueradiata*	Japanese amberjack
Hiramasa	All Japan	*Seriola lalandi*	Yellowtail amberjack
Hirenaga-kanpachi	All Japan	*Seriola rivoliana*	Almaco jack
Kanpachi	All Japan	*Seriola dumerili*	Greater amberjack
Kanpachi, "Kona"‡	Hawaii	*Seriola rivoliana*	Almaco jack

* Mature adult, generally weighing 11 pounds or more
†In Japan: young adult.In the United States: often applied to all sizes of all members of genus *Seriola*
‡Farmed and branded product

The vocabulary used to describe the Japanese amberjack in particular can be further broken down by age and location:

AREA	GROWTH STAGE OF *S. QUINQUERADIATA*				
	Fry	Juvenile	Young adult	Adult	Large adult
Noto Peninsula	*Mojako*	*Kozokura*	*Kando/Ganto*	*Buri*	
Kansai region	*Mojako*	*Tsubasu*	*Hamachi*	*Mejiro*	*Buri*
Kanto region	*Mojako*	*Wakashi*	*Inada*	*Warasa*	*Buri*
Kyushu Island	*Mojako*	*Wakanago*	*Hamachi*	*Mejiro*	*Buri*

Now, on to sustainability.

I know no one wants to hear it, but the *hamachi* (or *buri*, or *inada* ... you see where I'm going) that we all love so dearly is a cause for serious concern. The Japanese farming operations that raise these fish employ some questionable practices, which are likely having a negative impact on the local environment. First and foremost, hamachi is generally taken from the wild and reared in captivity, rather than being raised from an egg. This means that even though the fish are farmed, we are still taking them from the wild stocks. Every amberjack raised in a hamachi farm is one that will never have a chance to breed in the wild—and the wild stocks need those breeders. The exact causes are unknown, but wild hamachi populations have been in decline since the 1960s.

Hamachi farms in Japan also tend to stock their fish in high-density pens. This kind of aquaculture invites a significant risk of disease outbreak. Not only can these diseases be transferred to neighboring wild populations through escaped fish, but the disease threat is oftentimes countered with antibiotics, which can be passed on to the consumer.

To make matters worse, these farmed fish eat a lot of other fish. Farmed Japanese amberjack are often raised on sardines, and it can take up to eight pounds of sardines to get one pound of salable *hamachi*.

In Australia the farming operations aren't perfect, but they offer us a better option than the Japanese farms. *Seriola lalandi* is the species usually farmed in Australia, where it is called "kingfish" and marketed as either yellowtail or *hiramasa*. These farms are less troubling than their Japanese counterparts as they raise their fish from eggs rather

U.S. farmed **kanpachi,** *served on the rocks with a twist*

than recruiting them from wild stocks, and they use pellet feed instead of sardines (although the fish-in to fish-out ratio is still uncomfortably high). Fish density in Australian farms also tends to be lower than standard levels in Japanese farms.

Amberjack is also farmed in the United States. The U.S. product, which is usually *Seriola rivoliana*, is also superior to Japanese *hamachi* from an environmental standpoint. Strong regulations, thorough monitoring practices, and a closed life-cycle operation in which farmed fish are hatched from eggs rather than captured from wild stocks all serve to bolster this industry as a good alternative to farmed hamachi.

Wild *hamachi* from Japan is also available at sushi bars from time to time.

Recommendations:

U.S. farmed amberjack *(kanpachi)* is probably our best option, due to solid management, low levels of local impact, and thoughtful sourcing practices.

Australian farmed amberjack *(hiramasa)* is similar insofar as it spares wild stocks, uses low-density farms, and management practices seem to be sensitive to disease and parasite issues.

Wild *hamachi* from Japan is an open question. Stock strength continues to fall, perhaps due in part to the abduction of fry for *hamachi* farming operations. Caution is the watchword here.

Farmed Japanese *hamachi* is a poor choice. Due to its dependence on wild juveniles, reliance on high-density systems, and continual demand for large quantities of fish for feed, this is an option that is best avoided.

Amberjack is an enormous part of the U.S. sushi complex, rivaling such staples as tuna and eel. If we want to continue to enjoy it, we have to change our habits. Order *hiramasa* or *kanpachi* instead of *hamachi*, and as a general rule, eat less amberjack overall.

SOURCE	TYPE	
United States	Farmed	
Australia	Farmed	
Japan	**Farmed**	Wild

Mercury risk: **Unknown**

ARCTIC CHAR / *IWANA*

Salvelinus alpinus alpinus

Char, a close relative of trout and salmon, has only found its way onto U.S. sushi menus in the past few years. Char is known as *iwana* in Japanese. Its delicate red flesh and firm texture are quickly earning it a place in the American palate.

Arctic char is a cold-water fish inhabiting freshwater and saltwater areas in the far north of the planet. While wild arctic char populations in certain areas have been exploited for decades and may be in decline, a char farming industry has arisen in the last decade to meet the growing demand. Char are most often farmed in North America and Scandinavia, and most are raised in closed containment systems that do not expel waste into the surrounding environment. In contrast to the open systems used by most salmon farms, there are fewer problems associated with closed containment technology. Ocean water does not openly flow through these farms, so there is no danger of disturbing the genetic makeup of wild fish or parasite dispersal into nearby waters. Also, as char farms are popping up in many different areas, sushi bars can buy it locally and cut down on the distance your food has to travel.

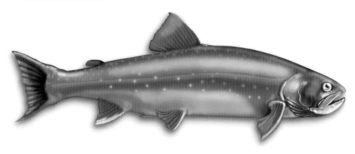

Arctic char farmed in a closed containment system is a delicious option at the sushi bar and a strong sustainable alternative to farmed salmon. Closed containment technology helps protect our environment and safeguard wild stocks.

Arctic char farmed in an open containment system is generally raised in open ponds. Such arrangements can threaten the surrounding ecosystem to some degree.

Wild arctic char is a less positive option. Some stocks in Europe and Canada have shown declines due to fishing and pollution, and others may be similarly threatened.

IWANA / ARCTIC CHAR

Arctic char offers us an incredible opportunity to replace farmed salmon with a much more sustainable product. If your local sushi bar doesn't offer arctic char, mention it to the chef.

SOURCE		
Wild		
Farmed	Open-containment	**Closed-containment**
Mercury risk: Low		

ATLANTIC MACKEREL / *SABA*

Scomber scombrus

Atlantic mackerel, or *saba,* is a schooling fish found throughout much of the Atlantic Ocean. It is one of the three types of mackerel most commonly found in sushi bars (the others are *aji* and *sawara*.) Of the three, saba is the most widely encountered option.

Mackerel does not keep well, and if it is not consumed within the first several hours after being caught, it may cause food poisoning. For this reason, the members of the mackerel family *(saba, aji,* and *sawara)* are the only fish traditionally salt-cured before being served as sushi.

Atlantic mackerel is caught in great numbers by the fleets of numerous countries. Although there have been concerns over stock strength in the past, especially in the waters around the British Isles, the U.S. domestic mackerel fishery is relatively well-managed. Moreover, it is supported by strong stocks and uses low-impact fishing gear, primarily mid-water trawls (large nets that do not touch the seabed).

Much of the imported European mackerel is not as sustainable as U.S. product due to a history of stock depletion. However, one foreign fish-

ery in particular does merit support: Mackerel caught with hand
lines in southwest England has
been certified by the Marine
Stewardship Council as a well-
managed, sustainable fishery.

It should be mentioned that
the term *saba* can also refer to
Scomber japonicus, the Pacific mackerel. Less is known about Pacific
mackerel fisheries than their Atlantic counterparts, but they benefit
from the same inherent resilience and low-impact catch methods that
make Atlantic *saba* such a positive option.

In general, domestic *saba* is a much more sustainable choice than
many other sushi options and can be enjoyed on a regular basis. It
also has the benefit of low mercury levels—a good thing for women
who are or will soon become pregnant.

SPECIES	SOURCE		
Aji (horse mackerel)	Domestic	Imported	
Saba (Atlantic mackerel)	Domestic	Marine Stewardship Council-certified imported	Other imported
Sawara (Spanish or king mackerel)			

Mercury risk: Low

BARRAMUNDI / *AKAME*

Lates calcarifer

Not a traditional sushi fish, the stocky hump-backed barramundi is a transplant from the coasts of Australia and the tropical straits of Indonesia and Papua New Guinea. It is quite rare to find barramundi on North American sushi menus, and it is included here largely to make a point to any curious chefs that happen to be browsing through this book: If it is raised responsibly, farmed barramundi can be one of the most sustainable seafood items one could hope for.

In the United States, barramundi is farmed in closed-containment facilities that pose no significant threat to the surrounding environment. Additionally, barramundi can be fed a diet very low in fish products, creating a net gain in protein. In fact, the metabolism of the barramundi enables it to synthesize omega-3 fatty acids (the same ones thought to improve brain development) from a heavily herbivorous diet.

Wild barramundi is not generally consumed in the United States, but that's probably not much of a loss. Stocks aren't well understood, es-

pecially within Indonesian and Papuan waters, and quality can vary significantly. More of a concern is barramundi raised in foreign farms. These operations can be problematic as they may be using open-containment systems that don't adequately address pollution risks or potential disease problems, and they may employ excessive amounts of fish products in their feeding protocol. Many farms—especially in Southeast Asia—are guilty on both counts.

QUICK FACT

The word 'barramundi' comes from the language of an aboriginal people in northeastern Australia. It means 'large scales.'

Barramundi is an excellent choice when it comes from a U.S. farm. Luckily, most barramundi found in North American sushi bars hails from this clean, well-managed domestic industry and is a delight to the palate. Try it in place of less sustainable *hirame* or *tai* options.

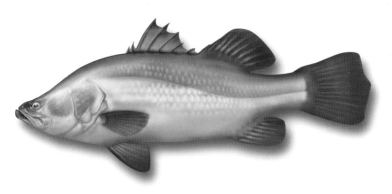

SOURCE		
United States		
Other	**Open-containment**	Closed containment
Mercury risk: Low		

Thunnus spp.

Tuna is the crown jewel of the sushi bar. Lean scarlet slices of *maguro* are a mainstay of the industry and one of the most popular sushi selections in the United States. Unfortunately, our ever-growing demand for tuna is beginning to have deleterious effects on the oceans.

The tuna is an impressive animal. It is a schooling fish of the open sea that can migrate thousands of miles through the oceans. Tuna are apex predators, voracious consumers of other fish and sea life. Some species, like the bluefin, can reach tremendous proportions: A mature bluefin tuna can outweigh a pony.

There are five species of tuna commonly found at the sushi bar. This section deals with yellowfin and bigeye, the two species commonly sold as *maguro*. The third species, bluefin, is discussed in the section on toro. The fourth species, albacore, is sold as *shiromaguro* and is also discussed in a separate section. The fifth species is skipjack tuna; see the section on *katsuo* (bonito) for more information.

Yellowfin tuna (*Thunnus albacares* is the backbone of the high-end tuna industry. It is generally caught with longlines (long ropes baited with hooks in series) or with gill nets, and often hails from the southern and western reaches of the Pacific. Although known as *kihada* in Japanese, it will be listed as *maguro* on U.S. sushi menus.

Thunnus albacares, the yellowfin tuna

MAGURO / BIGEYE AND YELLOWFIN **TUNA**

Yellowfin is found in the Pacific, Indian, and Atlantic oceans, and these distinct populations are under different amounts of pressure. The stock in the Atlantic is the healthiest and best understood, and it is not currently being overfished. The Pacific and Indian Ocean stocks, however, are being heavily exploited and populations are dwindling.

Bigeye tuna *(Thunnus obesus)* makes up a large portion of the sushigrade product in the United States. Chances are that if your *maguro* isn't yellowfin, it's bigeye. Bigeye is known as *mebachi* in Japanese but is almost never advertised as such.

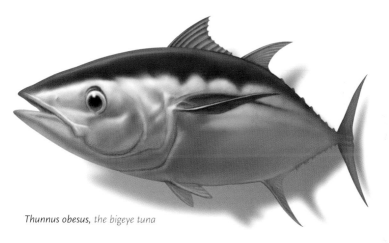

Thunnus obesus, the bigeye tuna

Bigeye stocks around the world are suffering under heavy fishing pressure. This species is generally caught in the tropical Pacific, and populations in this area are in the most trouble. In the eastern Pacific, for example, immature and juvenile bigeye comprise over fifty percent of the total catch.

An issue common to both bigeye and yellowfin tuna is the gear utilized to catch them. Longlines, purse seines, and trolled hand lines are all used to land these fish, and each has a different impact on the ecosystem. Hand lines are relatively precise in terms of targeting the species. Longlines, however, tend to have high levels of bycatch (unintended species and juveniles that are caught and discarded), thus indiscriminately killing turtles, sharks, seabirds, juvenile tuna, and other animals. Purse seines—a large net pulled around a school of fish, the ends joined into a circle, and then closed at the bottom—are generally better than longlines, but they too can be highly destructive. If boats using purse seines employ buoys and floats (known as fish aggregation devices or FADs) to concentrate schools of tuna, the bycatch problem is exacerbated and the level of damage increases.

Compared to bluefin, neither yellowfin nor bigeye are major mercury concerns. That being said, these are still long-lived fish at the top of the food chain. Due to their formidable appetites, they have the capacity to concentrate significant levels of mercury in their bodies. Small children and pregnant women may want to exercise additional caution.

The state of affairs is quite complex, but here are the basics:

U.S. Pacific and Atlantic troll- or pole-caught yellowfin are your best choices when ordering *maguro*. Populations are stable, they are not being overfished, and the use of hand lines has reduced bycatch to low levels.

U.S. Pacific and Atlantic longlined yellowfin is caught from strong tuna populations, but these fisheries can have high levels of bycatch.

Imported and U.S. Gulf of Mexico troll- or pole-caught yellowfin has low bycatch but draws from depleted populations. Some of these fisheries also have very little management in place.

Purse-seined yellowfin (except from the Indian Ocean, South America, and the Philippines) is a questionable compromise when considering stock strength (moderate), bycatch (moderate), and management (varying). It is better than some alternatives, but not great.

Purse-seined yellowfin from the Indian Ocean, South America, or the Philippines is an unacceptable option, with high levels of bycatch, lax management, and shaky stock strength.

Imported and U.S. Gulf of Mexico longlined yellowfin fleets target weak stocks and have an unacceptable level of bycatch. This is the worst of the yellowfin options.

Bigeye is slightly simpler:

Troll-caught U.S. Pacific and Hawaii bigeye is a strong choice due to effective management, low bycatch, and rebounding populations.

Troll-caught imported bigeye is a surprisingly sound choice, as these fisheries tend to operate with low bycatch levels, and bigeye stocks have shown reassuring trends in recent years.

Longlined bigeye from the U.S. Pacific and Hawaii incurs a higher level of bycatch than would be ideal, but management and stocks are strong.

All U.S. Atlantic bigeye is a source of concern due to weak stocks.

Imported longlined bigeye should be avoided. The fishery tends to incur high levels of bycatch and to put heavy pressure on stocks.

YELLOWFIN

SOURCE	CATCH METHOD	
U.S. Atlantic and Pacific	**Troll- and pole- caught, handlined**	Longlined Purse-seined
U.S. Gulf of Mexico	Troll- and pole- caught, handlined	**Longlined** Purse-seined
South America, Indian Ocean, the Philippines	Troll- and pole- caught, handlined	**Longlined** **Purse-seined**
Other sources	Troll- and pole- caught, handlined	**Longlined** Purse-seined

BIGEYE

SOURCE	CATCH METHOD	
U.S. Atlantic	Troll- and pole- caught, handlined	Longlined
U.S. Pacific	**Troll- and pole- caught, handlined**	Longlined
Imported	**Troll- and pole- caught, handlined**	**Longlined**

Bigeye mercury risk: **High**

Yellowfin mercury risk: Moderate

BLUEFIN TUNA BELLY / *TORO*

Toro. There's nothing quite like it. The soft delicate taste, the silky ethereal texture, the lingering hedonistic delight that resonates long after the delicate morsel has slipped softly down your throat.

It's an incredible dish. I love it, you love it, everyone loves it—but we are loving it to death.

Toro is the general term for the belly flesh of a tuna and can be divided into two main types: *chu-toro*, cut from the less fatty sides of the belly, and *o-toro*, the belly's supple and glorious center. The allure of o-toro is matched only by its price: It can easily be the most expensive item on a sushi menu.

While *toro* can be cut from any large tuna, the quintessential toro experience is associated with the majestic bluefin tuna, known as honmaguro or kuromaguro, the largest and most highly prized member of the tuna family. It is also the most expensive fish in the ocean: A single animal once fetched 174,000 dollars at Tokyo's Tsukiji fish market.

Price tags of such magnitude launch a lot of ships. The various bluefin species (*Thunnus thynuus, T. orientalis,* and T. maccoyii) are caught in both the Pacific and the Atlantic, and tuna fleets from dozens of countries pursue their quarry wherever it is found. The bluefin has been ruthlessly exploited to the point that stocks are on the verge of collapse.

Bluefin tuna populations in the western Pacific are estimated at less than ten percent of their virgin levels. Populations in the Atlantic are also in dire straits. To worsen matters, bluefin is generally longlined

O-toro nigiri: decadent, delicious—and environmentally devastating

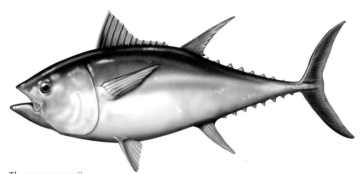

Thunnus maccoyii,
the coveted southern bluefin tuna

(caught on long ropes with thousands of baited hooks in series). As discussed in other chapters, this indiscriminately impacts many other animals. Hundreds of thousands of dead fish, seabirds, and turtles are discarded by bluefin tuna hunters every year.

The high market value of bluefin has given rise to an ominous new industry: the bluefin tuna ranch. These farms are unsustainable by their very nature. Farming bluefin is akin to farming tigers—top-of-the-food-chain carnivores who demand large amounts of protein. For every pound of tuna that comes out of a bluefin farm, twenty or more pounds of fish have gone in. Practicing aquaculture this high on the food chain is environmentally dangerous. Worse, these ranches typically capture wild juveniles and rear them rather than raising the fish from eggs. Until a better way of raising this fish is developed, it's best not to support this industry.

Bluefin is also a poor choice for those concerned about mercury. Very high levels of the metal have been found in both Atlantic and Pacific bluefin.

The bottom line is that bluefin is more than a delicacy—it is an essential but extremely vulnerable part of our ocean ecosystem. This is a fish that should be should be venerated and protected, not wiped from the face of the deep in a relentless crusade of greed and gluttony.

For yellowfin or bigeye, see the chapter on maguro *for rating information.*

SOURCE	
Farmed	
Wild	Atlantic, Pacific

Mercury risk: **Extreme**

BONITO / *KATSUO*

Sarda spp., Katsuwonus pelamis

Katsuo is one of those Japanese menu terms that can get the average American sushi lover into a bit of trouble. The word corresponds to two different fish: skipjack tuna (Katsuwonus pelamis; notice the similarity to *katsuo*) and bonito (Sarda spp.), a tuna relative in a different and distinct genus. The precise term for Sarda species is *hagatsuo*, but it is rarely employed on menus in the United States.

It's difficult to tell if the *katsuo* on the plate in front of you is skipjack or bonito. Both fish are often cooked or otherwise preserved before being served. Bonito does not freeze well and is not served raw due to its strong flavor. Instead it is usually seared and served with scallions and horseradish. For similar reasons, skipjack is often served the same way.

Bonito *sashimi*

Sarda chiliensis lineolata, the Pacific bonito

As a general rule, it much more common to encounter skipjack tuna than true bonito in a sushi bar. While there are certainly exceptions to this rule, information is often difficult to acquire because of the translation problem posed by the dual applications of the word katsuo. Unless there is reason to believe otherwise, it should be assumed that the katsuo in front of you is skipjack.

A great deal of bonito caught in Japan is dried and shredded into *katsuobushi* (bonito flakes), which is a very common ingredient in many Japanese dishes. Once dried and prepared in such a manner, bonito can be shipped anywhere in the world and remain palatable for an extended period of time.

True bonito may be facing trouble in the United States. It has slipped through cracks in the regulations: There are no real limits on the capture of bonito, and populations seem to have dwindled severely since the 1960s and 1970s. That being said, bonito is a migratory fish and supports a "pulse" fishery. Pulse fisheries occur when a species passes through an area only once in a while, attracts heavy fishing pressure when it is nearby, and then disappears altogether. So, some might argue that populations are still strong and the fish are just elsewhere for the time being. However, it has been some time since the last bonito "pulse" in U.S. waters.

There were once commercial boats in California that targeted bonito, but this fleet is now largely defunct. True Bonito found in the sushi bars of the United States are probably caught by trolling or incidentally by mackerel trawlers and other fleets.

Bonito populations may also be affected by "decadal oscillation," a phenomenon in which the ocean climate alternates between two extremes. This pattern affects the sardine and anchovy populations off the California coast. Anchovies are the preferred food of bonito, and the tiny fish are currently in decline due to a climate that favors sardines. If there is a shift toward anchovies in the near future, it is quite possible that it will bolster the bonito population substantially.

BONITO / *KATSUO* *continued*

True bonito from the US West Coast is from a poorly-understood fishery that may or may not be a sustainable option. The general lack of management is troubling, as is the absence of the fish from local waters in recent years. Californian bonito is now targeted primarily by a recreational fishery, so it is only rarely encountered in sushi bars."

As for skipjack tuna, it matures quickly, and populations are relatively strong—the major issue is how it is caught. Skipjack are targeted by longlines, which are miles-long ropes baited with hooks in series; purse seines, a large net pulled around a school of fish, the ends joined into a circle, and then closed at the bottom; and handlines or trolled lines. Each of these methods varies significantly in its impact on the ecosystem.

Longlined skipjack is known to have high levels of bycatch, unintended species and juveniles that are caught and discarded, including turtles and sharks. The only exception to this rule is the Hawaiian longline fishery, which has strict bycatch regulations.

Purse-seined skipjack fleets are generally less destructive to fish populations than longliners. However, many seiners use fish aggregating devices (FADs) to concentrate the catch. These man-made objects, often buoys or floats, attract many types of fish and are known to cause significant bycatch in these fisheries.

Skipjack prepared in classic nigiri style

Troll-caught skipjack has almost no bycatch and is an excellent choice at the sushi bar.

So, if your sushi bar offers *katsuo*, be sure to determine the species. Bonito could be a relatively sustainable option, but the jury is still out. Until there is management in place and we know more about the dynamics of the population, it's best to be cautious. Skipjack can be a good choice or a poor one depending on how it was landed.

QUICK FACT

Skipjack tuna acquired their name from their habit of leaping out of the water and effectively 'skipping' across the surface.

Katsuwonus pelamis, skipjack tuna

SPECIES	CATCH METHOD	SOURCE
Bonito		All
Skipjack	**Handlined**	All
	Purse-seined	All
	Longlined	Hawaii
	Longlined	Elsewhere

Mercury risk: Low

CAPELIN / *KARAFUTO-SHISHAMO*

Mallotus villosus

Masago is the processed roe (eggs) of the cape-lin, a small fish that exists in vast quantities throughout the northern Atlantic and Pacific oceans. It is generally orange-red in color and is often used as a garnish or to top pieces of nigiri. It should not be confused with *tobiko,* the roe of the flying fish, which is similar in color but more transparent and slightly larger.

Although the flesh of *karafuto-shishamo* is exceedingly rare at sushi bars, *masago* is a common ingredient. It can be a sustainable, dependable option, especially when compared with the more dubious *tobiko*—but it is important to differentiate the various sources of *masago*. This task isn't always easy as most *masago* is exported from Iceland or Canada to Taiwan or Japan for processing and then reexported to the United States. In such cases, the package often simply reads "Product of Taiwan" or "Made in Japan." Still, it's always worth asking the chef about the actual source. For the highly dedicated, it wouldn't hurt to get the name of the masago purveyor and look them up online after dinner; there's a vast amount of

Oscar's Art Books Broadway
1533 West Broadway Vancouver V6J1W6
(604)731-0553
GST# 125004598RT

www.oscarsartbookstore.com

Sat Jan23-10 4:47pm
Acct: AGELL00 Inv: 462890 G 00

Qty	Price Disc		Total Tax
9781556437694 Sustainable Sushi: A Guide			
1	17.95	20%	14.36 1

		Subtotal	14.36
		Tax GST	0.72
Items	1	Total	15.08
		Cash	20.00
		Change Due	4.92

Total Discount Savings: $3.59

====== Frequent Buyer Status ==========
Credit earned with this purchase $ 0.43
Total credit on your account.... $ 0.43
Minimum required for redemption..$ 5.00

No Refunds. Exchange or credit
note within 21 days with receipt.
Calendars may be exchanged for
calendars only - no credit value.
no credit,no exchange,no returns
for books with cds or dvds.

information on the Web pertaining to the world of sushi.

Icelandic *masago* is a good option at the sushi bar and can be readily enjoyed. Iceland is currently the world's largest harvester of capelin and capelin roe, and Icelandic fishing practices are well-managed with thoughtful precautions and little or no bycatch (animals caught unintentionally and discarded).

Canadian *masago* is also available but is a less desirable option. The Canadian capelin fishery is notoriously wasteful, landing large amounts of fish and systematically discarding all juveniles and adult males as useless for harvesting roe. Additionally, Canadian management practices and scientific efforts are not as strong as they could be.

Russian *masago* and **Norwegian *masago*** are not sustainable options. Historically, the largest capelin fishery in the world has been in the Barents Sea, the icy waters north of Norway and Russia. In 2004 this fishery was closed indefinitely due to alarmingly low stock levels. *Masago* from this area should be avoided until the stock stabilizes.

SOURCE
Iceland
Canada
Russia and Norway

Mercury risk: Low

CONCH / *SAZAE*

Strombas gigas

Conch (pronounced "konk") is finding its way into sushi bars across the United States and other countries. It is served as *nigiri*, in fried fritters, *sunomono*, and many other dishes. Unfortunately, no matter how it may be prepared, it is a cause for serious concern.

Sazae available in the United States is generally queen conch, a large marine snail that lives in the Caribbean Sea. This part of the world has numerous small independent island nations, many of which have questionable fishery management practices. Conch sales to the United States from the Dominican Republic, Haiti, and Honduras were suspended in 2003 due to an alarming crash in populations. While this policy reduced the pressure on the conch stocks in these countries, it increased them in neighboring nations like Jamaica and Turks and Caicos.

The conch is a long-lived animal that is easy to catch and produces fewer offspring than some other mollusks, such as the geoduck *(mirugai)*. These characteristics make it extremely susceptible to fishing pressure. Add this vulnerability to a general lack of fishery management (and a delicious reputation), and the conch's future starts to look bleak.

In some parts of the United States, the word *conch* can also refer to the knobbed whelk (*Busycon carica*), a different marine snail harvested

along the Eastern Seaboard. Knobbed whelk is sometimes referred to as "yellow conch." Unfortunately, there is no current management for the knobbed whelk, nor is there any such plan under development. In such a situation, we must be all the more conscientious.

Attempts at conch aquaculture are currently in the works, particularly in the Turks and Caicos Islands. This operation shows promise, but the product is difficult to find, and it's too early to tell how sustainable the enterprise will prove to be in the long run. For now it's best to simply give the conch a break and let the populations recover.

Fans of conch are encouraged to try more sustainable options, such as farmed abalone and farmed geoduck. If you must have conch, try to restrict your indulgences to very special occasions, and seek out farmed product.

SPECIES	SOURCE
Queen conch	Wild
	Farmed

Mercury risk: Unknown

CRAB / *KANI*

At the sushi bar, "crab" is a category rather than a single animal. Depending on how and where you order, you may receive king crab, snow crab, Dungeness crab, stone crab, blue crab, or even *surimi,* which isn't really crab at all. To make matters even more confusing, the crab may be from the United States, Canada, Russia, or Japan. Don't get discouraged, though—it's not as complicated as it seems.

King crab is usually considered the highest-quality crab available in the United States. These long-legged crustaceans stalk the depths of the northern Pacific and are harvested in Alaskan, Canadian, and Russian waters. All of these fisheries have had severe problems with habitat destruction and overfishing in the past.

Snow crab (or "queen" crab) is a common alternative to king and is similar in texture. Snow crab generally hails from Canada or Alaska.

Dungeness crab is rarely found outside the West Coast of the United States. It will almost always be specifically labeled "Dungeness" on the menu.

Stone crab is a small, thick-shelled crab from the southeastern United States. Rarely found at sushi establishments, its native waters are usually restricted to the Gulf of Mexico and the southern reaches of the Eastern Seaboard.

Blue crab (and the similar blue swimmer crab) is the ubiquitous crustacean most often used in "crab meat" dishes. It is generally caught in Asia or on the East Coast of the United States. Some sushi bars in New York, Maryland, and other Eastern states use American blue crab in sushi, but elsewhere it is usually imported from Asia. Blue crabs that have just molted are often served as **soft-shell crab** in spider rolls.

QUICK FACT

Extreme weather, towering waves, hypothermia, sleep deprivation, and torrential storms are just some of the potentially lethal challenges faced by an Alaskan king crab fisherman, whose job is considered to be one of the most dangerous on the planet.

Many sushi restaurants will also offer a product known as "imitation crab" made from pollock or other fish. See the *kanikama* section for more information on this creation.

So here's the breakdown:

King crab: Alaskan stocks are shaky at best, but Alaska is working on more effective management methods. Enjoy this crab in moderation, and choose it over **Russian king crab,** which is suffering from overharvesting, habitat destruction, and a general lack of management.

The coveted red king crab, **Paralithodes camtschaticus**

CRAB / *KANI* continued

Snow crab: Both Alaskan and Canadian stocks have been severely depleted in the past. New management practices are aimed at stabilizing stocks, but their effectiveness has yet to be demonstrated.

Dungeness crab: Strong populations coupled with effective management have created a resilient and productive fishery. When available, this is a delicious and sustainable choice.

Stone crab: When these crabs are harvested, only one claw is taken. The crab is then returned to the water to regenerate its limb. This is a strong fishery with a low mortality rate—a good option compared to king, snow, or blue crab.

Blue crab: Heavy fishing pressures, habitat destruction, and the loss of juveniles as bycatch (animals caught unintentionally and discarded)—especially in the Gulf of Mexico—have challenged the resilience of this fishery. The Maryland and Virginia fishery has lately been the source of grave concern, with senators from both states calling for emergency regulations to deal with alarming stock declines. In the case of soft-shell crab, try to avoid **imported blue swimmer crab.** Very little is known about blue swimmer fisheries, and it is unlikely that they offer crab populations or their habitats sufficient protection.

Crab can be a difficult issue at the sushi bar, so it's all the more important to discriminate between sustainable and unsustainable choices. Knowing the difference allows us to shift our demand to the fisheries that can support it and ease the pressure on those that are flagging.

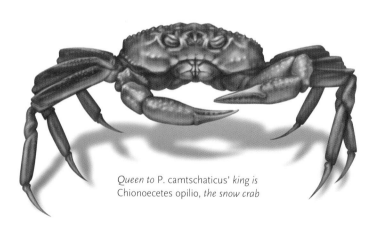

Queen to P. camtschaticus' *king is* Chionoecetes opilio, *the snow crab*

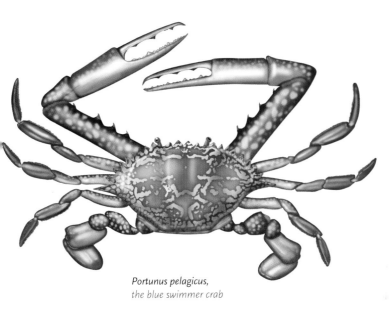

Portunus pelagicus,
the blue swimmer crab

SPECIES	SOURCE			
King crab	Alaska	Canada	Russia	Other sources
Snow crab	Alaska	Canada		
Dungeness crab	Washington	Alaska		
Stone crab	Any source			
Blue crab	United States	Imported		

Mercury risk: **Low**

ESCOLAR / *ABURASOKOMUTSU*

アブラソコムツ

Lepidocybium flavobrunneum

The escolar is a medium-sized ocean fish with a particularly high oil content and a dubious reputation. Caught in most of the planet's tropical and subtropical oceans, the escolar enjoyed a short-lived craze in the United States in the 1980s. It soon dropped off the radar for most seafood fans, but has now resurfaced courtesy of the sushi industry. Menus often label it "super white tuna," "butterfish," or "walu" (its Hawaiian name) and only rarely provide a Japanese translation. This is perhaps to avoid confusing customers with its incredibly laborious Japanese name, *aburasokomutsu*.

The consumption of escolar is riddled with potential problems. First off, the fish presents a health concern, as it contains very high levels of indigestible fatty acids and fatty alcohols known as wax esters. This can cause some degree of gastrointestinal discomfort in a significant percentage of people who eat it. Symptoms range from a slight queasiness to an incapacitating full-on colonic rebellion.

In addition to stomach burbles and potentially embarrassing after-dinner interruptions, those who would eat escolar should be aware of the problems in the fisheries. Escolar is landed all over the globe, but only U.S. fisheries are known to have any sort of management protocols or bycatch regulations (rules and catch limits on unintended species and juveniles that are subsequently discarded).

Few international fisheries specifically target escolar; it is generally caught incidentally on fishing longlines set for other species. Longlines are long ropes baited with hundreds of hooks in series. They have very high bycatch levels and have been known to entangle and kill other animals. Countless sea turtles, sharks, and seabirds have been killed by indiscriminate longliners. These international fisheries generally have no management in place. This means that little effort is made to minimize bycatch, and catch data is rarely confirmed by independent

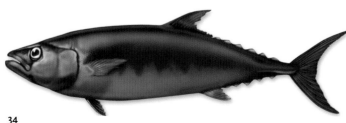

ABURASOKOMUTSU / ESCOLAR

observers. The bottom line? Unmanaged international longlining is emptying the oceans, and buying imported escolar supports the industry's negative practices.

The commercial sale of *aburasokomutsu* has been banned in Japan since 1977 due to the health issues discussed, and it is similarly prohibited in Italy. The United States, however, has no such forbearance, and many sushi chefs proudly serve escolar nigiri and sashimi on this side of the Pacific.

So, if readers are still interested in trying escolar, here's the breakdown:

Escolar from the United States is a better option than the imported product. Progressive management in Hawaii and the Atlantic has reduced bycatch levels, but there is still no strong understanding of stock strength. Proceed with caution.

Escolar from international sources is a bad idea. Ordering this fish promotes irresponsible practices that decimate fish populations, threaten endangered species, and support an opaque fishing regime. On top of it all, you're quite likely to get sick. It's best to pass on imported escolar.

SOURCE
Hawaii
U.S. Atlantic
International sources
Mercury risk: High

FLATFISH / *HIRAME* (PCB)

The term *hirame* can refer to just about any white-fleshed, horizontally oriented, bottom-dwelling fish: halibut, sole, flounder, fluke, turbot, and others. The key to enjoying *hirame* responsibly is to discern which particular fish is on your plate.

The best option we can hope for here in the United States is Pacific halibut *(Hippoglossus stenolipus)* from Alaska. With well-enforced regulations and thoughtful quota limits, this fishery has been a trendsetting example for progressive management and sustainable harvesting. That being said, decreasing population levels and increasing bycatch, unintended species and juveniles that are caught and discarded, are beginning to become issues in this fishery. The actual term for halibut in Japanese is *ohyo*.

If the fish is not Alaskan halibut, the issue starts to get more complicated. First of all, the names flounder and sole are thrown around very liberally and often can be misleading. True sole occurs only in the Atlantic. This doesn't prevent us from seeing Pacific Ocean "sole" for sale in the seafood market or finding "flounder" on a menu when what's actually being served is sole or turbot. There are even large-scale fisheries in the Pacific that target petrale and rex "sole," both of which are actually flounders. The technical Japanese term for flounder is *karei*.

ⓟ HIRAME / FLATFISH

The presence of California halibut on the West Coast doesn't
make the situation any simpler.
"California halibut" *(Paralichthys
californicus)* is actually a flounder, but nonetheless it is marketed as halibut. A large amount
of California halibut is caught
on longlines or bottom trawled
(caught in large nets dragged
along the sea bottom), but a
portion of the fishery employs
set nets that catch fish by their
gills and are known to entangle and kill other animals.

The big problem with many sole and flounder fisheries is the methods used to catch the fish. These fish are generally bottom-trawled: A
weighted net is dragged across the seabed to snare as many flatfish as
possible. Unfortunately, this kind of fishing causes a great deal of habitat disruption and can harm or kill other animals. This practice is especially troublesome in the Atlantic as the populations of many affected
species are already flagging.

So here's a quick cheat sheet to help decipher the thorniest parts of
the *hirame* issue:

Pacific halibut from Alaska is a good choice due to positive management and responsible fishing methods. Feel free to enjoy this species
as a staple item when you visit the sushi bar. This fish is rarely used for
sashimi and *nigiri,* but is commonly offered in cooked dishes.

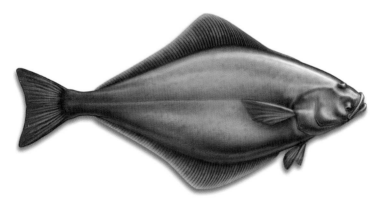

The imposing Pacific halibut, **Hippoglossus stenolipus**

FLATFISH / *HIRAME* *continued* (PCB)

Pacific flounder (or sole, or plaice, or turbot) is the runner-up. These species are generally bottom-trawled, but population levels seem to be healthier than in the Atlantic. This fishery is in delicate shape and calls for some moderation.

California halibut caught with a hook and line, or even a bottom trawl, is a reasonable choice, but not a great one.

Chilean flatfish are also beginning to enter the sushi industry for use as *hirame*. Unfortunately, very little is known about these populations and the way in which they are managed. It is best to be cautious until more is known.

California halibut caught with a set gill net doesn't merit our support. This fishery has a large amount of bycatch; marine mammals, such as the harbor porpoise, and numerous seabirds are often killed when they get entangled in these nets.

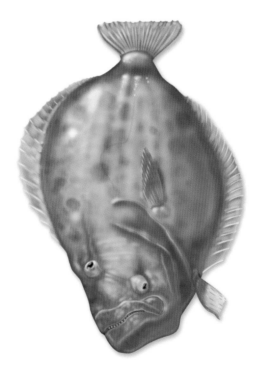

Paralichthys californicus, the
California halibut: not a real halibut

Atlantic sole (or fluke, or plaice) and Atlantic halibut are unsustainable choices due to destructive fishing practices and low population levels. If your sushi restaurant offers Atlantic flatfish as their *hirame*, try to order a more sustainable white fish, such as US farmed striped bass or barramundi. Alaskan *gindara* is also an excellent choice when available.

It's a complex issue, but with a few well-aimed questions we can recognize what's being offered as *hirame* and choose whether or not we want to support it.

Paralichthys dentatus, the summer flounder, often known as fluke

SPECIES	SOURCE		
Halibut	Alaska	Other sources	
California halibut	Hook and line	Bottom-dragged net	Gill net
Flounder, fluke, sole	Pacific	Atlantic	

Atlantic fluke mercury risk: Low

California halibut mercury risk: Moderate

Pacific halibut mercury risk: Moderate

FLYING FISH / *TOBIUO (TOBIKO)*

Simultaneously one of the most puzzling and beautiful creatures in the sea, the flying fish is in a class of its own. Well, technically, it's in a family of its own. Family *Exocoetidae* encompasses all of the fifty-odd species of flying fish, which are found throughout the world's temperate and tropical oceans.

Flying fish, or *tobiuo* in Japanese, is exceedingly difficult to find in a U.S. sushi bar. It is only included in this book because the roe of the flying fish, known as *tobiko,* is popular to the point of near ubiquity.

Naturally ranging from hazy orange to deep crimson, these tiny eggs are often dyed many other colors to accentuate the presentation of various dishes. They are often used for garnish, flavor, and texture, but are also sold on their own as *nigiri,* sometimes crowned with a raw quail egg (*uzura no tamago*).

Little is known about the health of the world's flying fish populations. These animals reproduce quickly and in large numbers. In some areas, such as the waters near Barbados, it is certain that heavy fishing has seriously affected local stocks. In other places, however, it is more difficult to tell. Flying fish are migratory by nature, and in certain areas various populations will mix and interbreed. Fisheries also do not differentiate between the various species of flying fish, but simply catch whatever type is available. Finally, to make matters even more complex, flying fish roe is harvested all over the world, transported to Japan or Taiwan for preparation (salting, curing, dyeing, etc.), and then reexported. As a result, the box containing *tobiko* at your local sushi haunt is likely to say "Product of Japan" or "Product of Taiwan," even though the eggs could be from anywhere.

Cheilopogon furcatus,
the spotfin flying fish

TOBIUO (TOBIKO) / FLYING FISH

In the absence of hard data and a transparent chain of custody, what do we do? *Sustainable Sushi* is based on the theory of the precautionary principle—when a resource isn't fully understood, it should be assumed to be limited rather than limitless. This notion is one of our greatest defenses against resource depletion and environmental degradation. The fact that we don't know much about the *tobiuo* fisheries is reason to be cautious, not to assume everything is fine. The science is still unclear on this one, so it's best to exercise moderation until we know more about the fishery.

If you have a real craving for roe, try Icelandic *masago*—it is very similar to *tobiko* and is known to be a strong sustainable option.

SPECIES	SOURCE
Tobiko	All

Mercury risk: **Unknown**

FRESHWATER EEL / *UNAGI*

Anguilla spp.

So many sushi fans love *unagi*, prepared on a grill and served with that delicious dark sauce, that it may be a bit painful to read this: Freshwater eel is one of the most environmentally destructive options at the sushi bar, and we need to cut back—way, way back.

These serpentine creatures were once almost completely unknown in the United States. Their consumption was restricted to small ethnic enclaves and unheard of in the general population. Times have changed; *unagi* is now one of the most popular choices in U.S. sushi bars.

Wild eel populations around the world are in severe decline. These population crashes stem from habitat alteration, overexploitation, climate change, pollution, and disease. Even as stocks plummet, however, the demand for freshwater eel continues to grow. As wild stocks have diminished, aquaculture has taken over. About ninety percent of the eel consumed in the United States is produced in farms, mainly in China, Taiwan, and Japan. Unfortunately, eel aquaculture tends to be sloppy and has a number of serious problems.

Fish meal: Eels are carnivorous. When these fish are kept in captivity, their keepers are forced to provide them with large amounts of protein. Regrettably, local wild fish stocks are often targeted for this purpose. Researchers estimate that 2.5 tons of wild fish are needed to produce a single ton of marketable eel.

Impact on wild populations: Most eel farms capture young eels from the wild and raise them in captivity rather than breeding them. That means that every eel raised by a farm is one that will never have a chance to reproduce in the wild. This is a serious problem, as the

world's eel stocks are in dire need of new breeders.

Escape and disease: Eels are adept at escaping from captivity. Most aquaculture systems that use modified wetlands and open systems see high numbers of fish escapes; eels in particular excel at wriggling their way out of captivity. This leads to cross-breeding between wild and domesticated stock, which can threaten future breeding patterns. Moreover, eels are suscep-

tible to many pathogens and can transfer diseases to wild populations when they escape from aquaculture facilities.

Anguilla japonica,
the Japanese freshwater eel

Wetlands destruction: Eel farms are often located in coastal wetlands. Most use open-tank systems that flush farm waste into the surrounding areas, which causes pollution and threatens local ecosystems.

The first step to improving this industry is to demand eel produced in farms with recirculating, or "closed," tank systems. Such farming techniques limit potential escapes and environmental damage. Until closed systems become the norm in eel aquaculture, we need to bring the demand for eel down to sustainable levels. Until the freshwater eel aquaculture industry cleans up its act, try to refrain from ordering *unagi*. If you must have eel, consider ordering *anago* (conger eel).

SOURCE
Wild
Farmed
Mercury risk: Low

GEODUCK / *MIRUGAI*

Panopea abrupta

First of all, *mirugai* is not giant clam, ocean clam, or long-neck clam, regardless of what the menu may say. *Mirugai* is geoduck, pronounced "goo-wee-duk," taken from a Nisqually Indian word meaning "to dig deep." A large burrowing bivalve native to the Pacific Northwest, this animal can reach upwards of ten pounds and live for over a century.

These immense clams live about three feet under the sand for their entire adult lives. Harvesters dig them up using a high-pressure water wand or an open-ended can and a shovel.

Historically, the demand for geoduck has been concentrated in Asia, where one plate of the delicious mollusk can fetch as much as a hundred dollars. Lately, however, the U.S. market for geoduck has exploded, due in no small part to increased demand in sushi bars.

There are two main sources of geoduck—Washington State and British Columbia. Both fisheries have wild and farmed components. Wild geoduck is harvested in Alaska as well, but on a smaller scale.

Wild geoduck stocks have fluctuated in the past but are generally strong. Management techniques vary between US and Canadian fisheries, but overall they have been effective in protecting the stock health and regulating exploitation. When available, wild geoduck is a solid choice at the sushi bar.

Farmed geoduck looks to have a promising future as well. Although there are some problems and unanswered questions, mainly having to do with geoduck genetics, farmed geoduck seems to be much more sustainable than its wild counterpart. Farmed geoduck spares standing wild populations, disturbs fewer tide-flat and seabed areas, and creates less bycatch, or unintended species and juveniles that are caught and discarded.

Geoduck farms are superior to many other types of aquaculture in that they don't use fish meal, antibiotics, or any other dietary supplements.

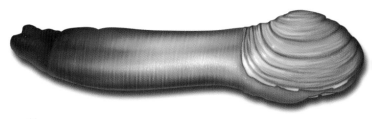

MIRUGAI / GEODUCK

Geoducks are filter-feeding herbivores and subsist entirely on algae that wash over their burrows when the tide comes in.

Geoduck is a good option at the sushi bar. As a step toward a healthier ocean, consider ordering *mirugai* instead of surf clam, wild abalone or conch, which are similar in taste and texture but far less sustainable.

SOURCE

Farmed

Wild

Mercury risk: **Low**

GIZZARD SHAD / *KOHADA*

Konosirus punctatus

The gizzard shad (or dotted gizzard shad) is a small fish related to the herring. *Konosirus punctatus* schools in great numbers along the shores of Central Japan, in the waters off eastern China, and around the Korean Peninsula. A mainstay of *edomae* (Tokyo-style) sushi, this fish is extremely popular in the Kanto region of Japan. It falls under the *hikari mono* (roughly translated as "shiny fish") category, which also includes *aji, iwashi, sanma,* and other fish served with their silvery skins intact.

While usually labeled *kohada* on sushi menus, this fish actually has a number of names, each corresponding to the age of the animal. Young gizzard shad are known as *shinko*. As the fish matures, its name becomes *kohada*, then *nakazumi*, and finally *konoshiro*, a fully grown gizzard shad.

Interestingly, the price of gizzard shad has an inverse relationship to its age. *Shinko* commands a much higher price than older shad—often over

KOHADA / GIZZARD SHAD

one hundred dollars per pound. This decrease in value is due to the fact that as the fish ages it becomes increasingly bony.

Such a pattern in demand calls for caution. As with many species of fish, female gizzard shad become capable of producing more eggs as they grow older. Every spawning season that these fish spend in the water helps bolster their population strength. Heavy fishing pressure on the young fish reduces the resilience of the fishery as a whole.

Moreover, not much is known about the current health of this fishery. Gizzard shad are usually caught in trap nets, which are anchored on the sea bottom, and beach seines, which are large bag nets operated from shore, but little information is available about any associated issues of bycatch, unintended species and juveniles that are caught and discarded. Gizzard shad populations are probably somewhat protected by rapid maturation and a high rate of reproduction, but not enough scientific information is available to make any solid recommendations.

Kohada offers us a good opportunity to apply the precautionary principle: Be careful with your consumption of this fish until more is known.

SPECIES	SOURCE
Kohada	All

Mercury risk: **Unknown**

HALFBEAK / *SAYORI*

Hyporhamphus sajori

The Japanese halfbeak, or needlefish, is one of the oddest animals ever to grace the sushi counter. With their long slender bodies and what is perhaps the most pronounced underbite in the animal kingdom, this fish looks more like a writing implement than a food source. Even so, the halfbeak is a coveted item, and they are hauled out of the water in large masses to appease sushi patrons from New York to Nagasaki.

Sayori are found from the Yellow Sea east of Korea to the waters off Eastern Siberia, but historically they have been caught along the southern coasts of Japan. They occur in large schools and are caught in the late winter and spring. A similar fish, *Hemiramphus spp.,* is caught in Florida and the Gulf of Mexico. It is also known as halfbeak, but it is not used by the sushi industry.

Sayori is just beginning to gain recognition in the United States, but it has been a traditional Japanese dish for centuries. In Japan the halfbeak is associated with the onset of spring and is served in a variety of forms, sashimi and nigiri being two of the most popular.

SAYORI / HALFBEAK

Very little is known about the health of the Japanese halfbeak fishery. We can take some comfort in the fact that the halfbeak is a small fish, almost never exceeding one foot in length, that matures quickly and breeds in large numbers. Still, without strong scientific data, it is irresponsible to claim that the fishery is sustainable. In fact, it has been all too common for fish like these, with their seasonal resurgences and seemingly limitless bounty, to be exploited into oblivion.

At this point, *sayori* is probably a better choice than many other items at the sushi bar. It is generally better to consume fish that eat low on the food chain, grow quickly, and die young rather than fish that eat at the top of the ecosystem, mature slowly, and live for many years. For example, it's theoretically better to eat sayori than bluefin tuna. That being said, without a solid understanding of management and fishery dynamics, we must exercise temperance—enjoy *sayori* in moderation.

SOURCE
All

Mercury risk: Unknown

HORSE MACKEREL / *AJI*

Trachurus spp.

Aji, also known as horse mackerel or sau-rel, is one of the three types of mackerel commonly available in sushi bars, the others being *saba* and *sawara*. The term *aji* refers to any member of the horse mackerel family. When aji is ordered in a U.S. sushi bar, what often arrives at the table is a tasty sample of Atlantic horse mackerel, or *Trachurus trachurus*. In Japan, however, *aji* is likely to mean *ma-aji*, or "true *aji*," a different species of horse mackerel (*T. japonicus*). One may also encounter ma-aji in high-end U.S. sushi bars, especially on the West Coast. Also, be aware that *aji* may be advertised as "Spanish mackerel," but true Spanish mackerel is actually called *sawara*.

The various species of horse mackerel are found in temperate areas throughout the world's oceans. They are generally caught with gill nets, which don't cause a lot of habitat damage. However, such methods do cause some bycatch, unintended species and juveniles that are

AJI / HORSE MACKEREL

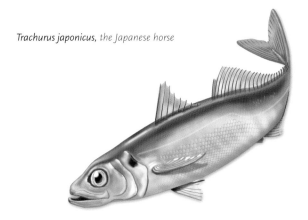

Trachurus japonicus, the Japanese horse

caught and discarded, and have been known to entangle and kill marine mammals from time to time.

Horse mackerel stocks are thought to be strong, and the U.S. fishery is under solid management. Less is known about imported mackerel, but the vast majority of the *aji* consumed in the United States is caught by U.S. fishing vessels. Chances are the aji in your local sushi establishment is domestic, but it's always a good idea to ask.

Aji is a good choice at the sushi bar due to its innate resistance to fishing pressure, effective management, and strong populations. Also, this fish is not known to contain the same mercury levels as Spanish or king mackerel. For women who are pregnant or planning to become so, aji is a better choice than sawara.

SPECIES	SOURCE		
Aji (horse mackerel)	Domestic	Imported	
Saba (Atlantic mackerel)	Domestic	Marine Stewardship Council-certified imported	Other imported
Sawara (Spanish or king mackerel)			
Mercury risk: Low			

IMITATION CRAB / *KANIKAMA*

Imitation crab (*surimi*) is used in many types of *maki*, or rolls. The most common example is the California roll, which generally contains imitation crab and avocado.

A fish processor creates imitation crab from *surimi*: a blend of fish, starch, sugar, and preservatives. This *surimi* is then formed into long rectangular shapes with red sides, known as *kanikama*. The result is a flaky, slightly sweet product that somewhat resembles crab in texture, appearance, and flavor. Alaskan pollock (*Theragra chalcogramma*) is the fish most commonly used to create imitation crab, and it is used in approximately fifty percent of global *surimi* production. The remaining product may contain threadfin bream, Pacific whiting, Japanese pollock, or other kinds of fish. Even though   contains no crab, it is often labeled as such, especially in lower-quality establishments or grocery store sushi items.

Imitation crab can actually be one of the most sustainable options at the sushi bar. When sourced from a well-managed fishery, *kanikama* can be an environmentally friendly option that is low in mercury. Also, supporting this industry can help ease the pressure on many of our flagging crab stocks.

There is one potential problem that must be mentioned—the unintentional catch of salmon in the pollock fishery. The percentage of salmon caught in this manner is small, but the sheer

KANIKAMA / IMITATION CRAB

size of the pollock industry—the second largest fishery in the world—means that even a small percentage represents a significant amount. In 2006, for example, 130,000 chinook salmon were discarded by the pollock fishery. Numbers like these have caused concern among some environmental groups and Alaskan salmon fishers. This being said, the Alaskan pollock fishery is taking measures to minimize bycatch (unintended species and juveniles that are caught and discarded).

Theragra chalcogramma, the Alaskan pollock

Alaskan pollock *surimi* is a good choice at the sushi bar. The fishery is well-managed and certified by the Marine Stewardship Council, and the pollock themselves are staggeringly abundant in number. Processed pollock may not have the appeal of king or snow crab, but it is a more sustainable option.

Surimi from other sources is a more dubious selection. Some fisheries have fewer regulations, and any number of other species may be affected, or even included in the processed product. It's better to stick to *surimi* made from Alaskan pollock, an actively managed and well-understood fishery, than to take a chance on a potentially much more destructive option.

SOURCE
Alaskan pollock
Other sources

Mercury risk: Low

MONKFISH / *ANKO (ANKIMO)*

Lophius americanus

Although not overly common in the United States, monkfish—and more often, monkfish liver *(ankimo)*—is certainly available in many upscale establishments. Monkfish liver is similar to a fine pâté in texture and is often smoked or steamed and served with scallions, daikon radish, and red-pepper sauce *(momiji oroshi)*. Monkfish is also known as goosefish or angler fish.

Monkfish was once considered a trash fish—no doubt partially due to its frightening appearance—and has only recently become acceptable to the American palate. Most monkfish served in the United States hails from the western reaches of the Atlantic Ocean, where it has been severely overfished in recent years due to increased demand. Bold management techniques in the Atlantic have relieved some of the pressure on monkfish populations, but it will take years for the species to fully recover.

ANKO (ANKIMO) / MONKFISH

Monkfish are generally harvested using bottom trawls—a fishing method that involves dragging a weighted net along the sea floor. This type of fishing is unnecessarily destructive to the local habitat and indiscriminate in which species and sizes of fish are ensnared.

Many people find monkfish delicious—I am one of them. Unfortunately, due to a history of overly aggressive fishing practices, eating this delicacy on any kind of regular basis is not a responsible option. If we want to enjoy monkfish ten, twenty, and thirty years from now, we must decrease our demand on the stocks and allow them time to recover. Give *ankimo* a miss.

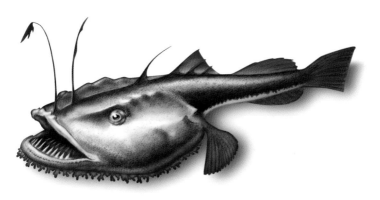

SOURCE

U.S. Atlantic

Mercury risk: Low

MUSSELS / *MUURUGAI*

Although it's rare to find mussel *nigiri,* many sushi bars offer a baked mussel special or appetizer. Order it. With so many questionable fisheries out there, it's refreshing to find one that truly merits our support.

The vast majority of the mussels we eat are farmed and come from all over the temperate world. Mussels are raised from larvae that is collected from the wild and then reared in suspended cages or along the seabed. There is no bycatch in this fishery aside from the larvae of other bivalves that may be incidentally taken along with the mussel larvae.

Farmed mussels require no fish meal; they take all of the protein they need from the water around them. In fact, they provide a valuable service to the ecosystem by removing debris and nutrients from the water through a filter-feeding process. In essence, seawater is cleaner after moving through a mussel farm—the exact opposite result of other more destructive types of aquaculture.

Mussels are rarely associated with diseases or pathogens, and no known parasites found in

farmed mussels are considered harmful to wild stocks or to consumers. Moreover, most mussel farms raise species that are native to their locales, which reduces potential environmental problems even further. New Zealanders farm green mussels, U.S. farms lean toward blue mussels, and Mediterranean mussels are popular in southern Europe. Although there are certainly exceptions to this trend, there has never been any evidence of genetic perturbation or crossover to wild mussels.

This is not to say that mussels cannot be an invasive species. The zebra mussel is notorious for this very characteristic, and it has spread from Asia to freshwater lakes and rivers around the world. However, this species is not used by the seafood industry and is not raised in any commercial mussel farms; there is no connection between the zebra mussel issue and the mussels at your favorite sushi restaurant.

In summary, farmed mussels are one of the best possible options at a sushi bar. They are a straightforward and refreshing exception to the often troubling trends within the sushi industry.

SOURCE

All

Mercury risk: **Low**

OCTOPUS / *TAKO* PCB

Octopus vulgaris

One of the most easily identifiable items at the sushi bar is the dimpled purple and white *tako*. *Tako* is prepared octopus, usually of the species *Octopus vulgaris* (*madako* in Japanese). Unlike many fish that are offered raw, octopus is cooked and brined before it is served as sushi.

Japan has a large octopus preparation industry. Octopus from all over the world is exported to Japan, where it is prepared and frozen. It is then reexported to sushi establishments in the United States, Europe, and elsewhere. Because of these convoluted travel plans, discovering where your octopus came from can be a difficult task. It is an important one, however, because the practices of these fisheries vary widely. The vast majority of the *tako* served in U.S. sushi bars was hauled out of the waters along the North African coast, but the many arms of the octopus complex stretch all over the globe.

Spain: There is an octopus fishery in the Mediterranean; some of the product from this area reaches Japan after being caught by the Spanish octopus fleet. The Spanish fishery seems well-managed when compared with African and Vietnamese fisheries. Additionally, a large portion of Spanish octopus is caught with pots, a much less disruptive process than bottom trawling, which involves dragging large nets along the sea bottom. Spanish bottom-trawled octopus is a questionable option due to the negative impact of the trawl nets; Spanish pot-caught octopus is the best possible option at the sushi bar for the *tako* aficionado, but it is extremely difficult to find.

Japan: Just to confuse matters, there is actually a domestic octopus fishery in Japan. Little is known about this fishery, but some efforts to protect stocks and restore damaged habitat have been made. Both

pots and bottom trawls are used to some degree. The pots are probably a better method, but it's nearly impossible to tell how a particular Japanese octopus was caught.

Morocco: Historically, the world's most important octopus fisheries have been off the coast of Morocco. The Moroccan octopus fishery has a turbulent past; populations have declined and bottom trawling has led to widespread habitat destruction. The trawling continues, but stocks have more protection now: Morocco has initiated some fishing closures—periods when the beds are off-limits to fishing—to safeguard its octopus populations. Whether or not these policies will be effective in the long run remains to be seen.

Mauritania and Senegal: Morocco's neighbors are also in on the action—Mauritania and Senegal have octopus fisheries, but they seem to be operating under little regulation. Mauritanian stocks in particular may be declining and are poorly understood. Octopus from these countries is not a sustainable option.

Vietnam: Vietnam is known to export octopus to Japan for preparation, but Vietnamese fishing methods are unregulated and stocks are thought to be suffering. Vietnamese octopus is best avoided.

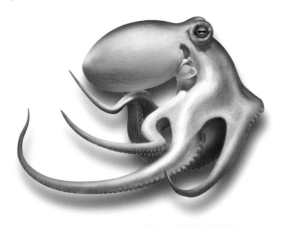

SOURCE
Spain
Morocco
Mauritania
Senegal
Japan
Vietnam

Mercury risk: Low

OYSTERS / *KAKI*

Oysters are becoming more and more common on menus in U.S. sushi restaurants. These bivalves are presented in a variety of forms and styles: roasted in the shell, raw on the half shell, or glistening with *ponzu* sauce, yuzu-soy reductions, or any of a thousand other delectable touches.

On a global scale, about ninety-five percent of the oysters we eat are farm-raised. The United States boasts a large number of oyster farms along its coasts, as do Canada, Japan, and many other countries. Oysters are comparatively easy to raise and of high value, so many fish farmers have invested in this industry.

Luckily for us, farmed oysters are also one of the more sustainable options at the sushi bar. As filter feeders, not only do they not require feed added to the water, they actually clean their surrounding habitat by converting nutrients and organic matter into consumable biomass.

When farmers import a foreign strain of oysters, there is a potential problem that can occur. Oysters, like many bivalves, are broadcast spawners; sexually mature oysters emit thousands of reproductive cells into the surrounding waters. When an alien species of oyster is introduced to a new habitat, it may disturb the genetic makeup of native species, or even cause a bioinvasion.

Wild oysters are a different matter. Unless they are from an artisanal fishery (that involves skilled operators but is small and not industrialized) and gathered by hand, it is likely that they were obtained by dredging. Some forms of dredging tear up great swathes of sea floor

in order to capture the creatures dwelling in or on it. Needless to say, this practice can be incredibly detrimental to the environmental health of any given area.

In general, farmed oysters are an excellent choice at the sushi bar. Consider making them one of your staple items when you visit your favorite sushi restaurant.

SOURCE

Farmed

Wild

Mercury risk: Low

SABLEFISH / GINDARA

Anoplopoma fimbria

A relative newcomer to the U.S. sushi scene, sablefish—also called black cod—is a longtime favorite in Japan, where it is known as *gindara*. The species is also sometimes identified as butterfish, although this term can also refer to escolar, a completely different animal. If the menu advertises butterfish, ask the chef where it comes from—if the answer is Alaska, Canada, or the West Coast of the United States, it's sablefish. For all other geographical sources, see the section on escolar (*aburasokomutsu*).

Sablefish is caught along the North American coast from the Bering Sea to Baja California. Most of this catch has historically ended up in Tokyo sushi restaurants, where the delicate white flesh of the sablefish is prized for its flavor and texture. Consumer demand put some serious fishing pressure on stocks in the 1970s and 1980s, and for a time the strength of populations was a concern. Luckily, they seem to have rebounded in the past decade.

Sablefish is generally caught on longlines, which are long ropes baited with hooks in series, but bottom trawls (large nets dragged along the sea bottom) and traps are also employed in certain areas. Some fish farms in British Columbia are beginning to raise sablefish as well.

Longline and trap-caught sablefish from Alaska and British Columbia is an excellent choice. These fisheries use relatively benign catch methods—even the longline operations seem to have only minor impacts on other animals—and have been certified by the Marine Stewardship Council. Moreover, these organizations boast strong management, effective enforcement protocols, and healthy populations.

Bottom-trawled sablefish from Alaska and British Columbia draws from the same strong and well-managed populations, but has higher levels of bycatch, unintended species and juveniles that are caught and discarded, and can damage the surrounding environment. Still a good choice, but not as good as the trap-caught alternative discussed above.

Farmed sablefish from Canada is more mysterious. Sablefish farming is a new industry, and its effects on the environment and on wild sablefish populations are not yet well understood. Additionally, due to unanswered questions regarding possible habitat impacts, there is opposition to these farms among environmentalists and scientists. Caution is encouraged until more is known.

Sablefish from Washington, Oregon, and California is a decent option, but not as good as wild Alaskan or Canadian sablefish. Much of the fleet in these more southern states tends to rely on bottom trawls, and the management is not as rigorous as it could be.

For the most part, *gindara* is a safe and enjoyable option at the sushi bar. Consider substituting it for less sustainable whitefish like *tai* or Atlantic *hirame,* or for whitefish from poorly understood fisheries like wild *suzuki.*

SOURCE	CATCH METHOD		
Canada	**Wild**	Farmed	
Alaska and Canada	**Longlined**	**Trapped**	Bottom-trawled
Other sources			
Mercury risk: Low			

SALMON / *SAKE*

Oncorhynchus spp., Salmo spp.

Salmon is the single most popular choice among U.S. sushi patrons. Unfortunately, it can also be a dangerous option. As conscientious consumers, this is one issue where we need to make our preferences known.

The last decade has seen a flood of farmed salmon entering the market. These farmed fish pose a threat to our health and to ocean ecosystems in a myriad of ways.

Feed: Salmon need meat and protein to survive. Sadly, feed providers often round up vast numbers of smaller fish, grind them into fish meal, and sell it to fish farmers. Such tactics can lay waste to fish populations. Moreover, it takes anywhere from two to four pounds of feeder fish to raise one pound of salmon. By farming animals that eat so high on the food chain, we're consuming more fish than we realize.

Waste and Pollution: The waste generated by a salmon farm is usually released directly into the ocean. This can be a problem for sensitive organisms living in nearby areas, especially sponges, corals, and other animals that are unable to move to cleaner waters.

Escape and Crossbreeding: An escape-proof salmon aquaculture system has yet to be implemented on any significant scale. Without such a system, some fish are always going to get away. In some cases these fugitives can crossbreed with wild fish and alter the local gene pool, threatening the next generation's ability to hunt and spawn.

Disease and parasites: The crowded conditions of farmed salmon increase their chances of contracting diseases or parasites. Unhealthy farmed fish can transmit parasites like sea lice to neighboring wild fish,

Even in appearance, there is a striking contrast between wild (left) and farmed salmon.

which threatens the strength of native salmon. Recent research suggests the severe sea lice problem in British Columbia could wipe out certain native populations in less than five years. Also, farmers sometimes use antibiotics or pesticides to combat these problems, and the residual chemicals can be passed on to consumers.

Some salmon farms are better than others, but no farms have yet adequately addressed all these problems to the point of meriting our unconditional support. Luckily, there is a simple way to enjoy salmon at the sushi bar and still vote for a healthier planet: Ask for wild salmon.

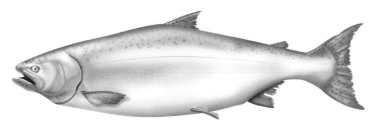

The majestic king salmon, **Oncorhynchus tshawytscha**

Wild salmon from Alaska have aggressive and fairly effective fishery management programs. Alaskan king (chinook), silver (coho), and sockeye (red) salmon all come from large fisheries much more sustainable than their farmed counterparts. Washington, Oregon, and California also boast salmon fisheries, but stocks are shaky and have been the source of much recent concern.

Wild salmon will probably come at a higher price than the farmed alternative at your local sushi establishment. It's important to remember, though, that consumer demand has an incredible impact on what options are available to the public. If a chef hears enough patrons demand wild sustainable salmon, he or she may add it to the menu in place of farmed fish.

Another excellent replacement for farmed salmon is farmed arctic char. A red-fleshed relative of the salmon, arctic char are usually raised in low-impact closed-containment farms where they pose no threat to the surrounding environment. See the *iwana* chapter for more information.

	TYPE	SOURCE	
(PCB)	Farmed		
	Wild	Alaska	Other sources

Mercury risk: **Low**

SARDINES / *IWASHI*

Sardinops sagax

Historically, the sardine has been a ubiquitous food fish. Although they are served in the best restaurants in Lisbon (Portugal is known for its sardines), in the United States sardines have traditionally been relegated to back alleys and whistle-stops. A staple of our seafood diet for decades, the sardine has usually been viewed as a "low class" fish fit merely for workmen's sandwiches and recognized only for having once powered the now-defunct canneries of Monterey, California.

The sardine has had rough times since Steinbeck's *Cannery Row*. When sardine stocks crashed in the mid twentieth century, the canneries closed and the boom ended. Luckily, this dearth of fishing pressure gave the sardine population time to recover.

Although the Japanese have traditionally used sardines in sushi, we are only just beginning to do so in the United States. As a result, it's still relatively uncommon to see *iwashi* on the menu at your local sushi bar. Only in the last few years have Americans begun to recognize the sardine as a tasty sushi fish.

IWASHI / SARDINES

As discussed, Pacific sardine stocks have been shaky in the past. However, thanks to solid management and an inherent resilience to fishing pressure, the species has recovered and populations are currently very strong.

Less is known about sardines from other parts of the world.

While they may be safe options, it's best to exercise caution. If given the choice, choose U.S. Pacific sardines over imported products.

It should be mentioned that a number of scientists have theorized the existence of a "decadal oscillation"—a kind of back-and-forth pendulum effect between the populations of two species of fish in a given area. Off the Pacific coast of the United States, studies suggest that sardines and anchovies alternate in prevalence every thirty to forty years. Currently, the climate and state of the waters seem to favor the sardine at the expense of the anchovy. Should conditions change, sardine stocks may be affected. Right now, however, *iwashi* from the Pacific coast of the United States is an excellent option at the sushi bar.

SOURCE

U.S. Pacific

Other sources

Mercury risk: Low

SAURY / *SANMA*

Cololabis saira

The Pacific saury is a skinny little stripe of silver that occurs in great multitudes along the coasts of the Pacific Ocean. It can be found in the seas around Japan, off the northeast coast of Russia, across the Bering Sea to the Gulf of Alaska, and southward as far as Mexico. These little fish grow quickly, reproduce in large numbers, and are an important food source for many ocean predators.

Sanma is very much a feast-or-famine fish, as it migrates and is generally either present in great numbers or conspicuously absent. When it migrates inshore, it is heavily targeted for fishing. This relative of the needlefish is the base of numerous seasonal dishes in Japan. It is especially popular in autumn.

In the United States, *sanma* is still relatively unknown. It may rotate through the specials board of a high-end sushi bar during the appropriate season, but it has not yet achieved a strong following.

At this point, there is little information on which to base a recommendation re-

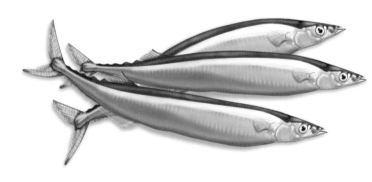

garding *sanma*. It's true that the fish is somewhat succored by its rapid growth rate, prolific abundance, and early onset of sexual maturity. It is important to remember, though, that these were also all characteristics of the passenger pigeon as well.

Enjoy *sanma* responsibly. While it is likely a better choice than many other less resilient fish, try not to order it too often until more is known about the dynamics of the fishery and the species' overall sustainability.

SOURCE

All

Mercury risk: Low

SCALLOPS / *HOTATE (HOTATEGAI)*

Scallops hold a place of honor not just at the sushi bar but to the American palate in general. Revered for their rich delicate flesh, scallops add a touch of decadence to many different types of cuisine.

The major market distinction for this bivalve is size—large scallops are sold as "sea scallops," while their smaller brethren are labeled "bay scallops." There are over three hundred species within the scallop family *(Pectinidae)*, but only about fifteen are used in commercial aquaculture; Patinopecten yessoensis, the Japanese or Yesso scallop, dominates the industry. It is large and is sold as a "sea scallop." Bay scallops are usually *Argopectens irradians,* a species primarily farmed in China.

Sushi chefs tend to favor large cold-water scallops from the coasts of Hokkaido for their premium dishes (such as live scallop *sashimi*). Both farmed and wild scallops come from this area. For other dishes, such as the popular spicy scallop roll, chefs may use less expensive products (like bay scallops).

The variables involved in appraising a scallop's sustainability are (1) the size, (2) the area where it was caught or raised, and (3) whether or not the scallop was farmed. Additionally, for farmed scallops, it's important to discern if the animal was suspension-farmed (reared in cages or on platforms suspended above the seabed) or bottom-cultured (planted along the seafloor and subsequently harvested.) If you can obtain this information, making a responsible decision is relatively simple.

HOTATE (HOTATEGAI) / SCALLOPS

Here's a quick breakdown of how scallops can be evaluated:

Farm-raised bay scallops are rarely used in sushi bars, but when available they are a good option. They are generally raised in low-impact suspension systems and require no significant amount of feed or additives.

Farm-raised sea scallops are also a good choice as long as they are **suspension farmed.** These large bivalves bring all the delicacy and elegance to a dish without relying on destructive catch methods.

Sea scallops raised on bottom farms are a more dubious choice. Harvesting bottom-farm scallops can involve some habitat disruption, as the seabed must be manipulated during the process.

Wild-caught sea scallops from Asia are also a questionable option. So little is known about stock strengths and population dynamics that it is impossible to determine if they are being or have already been overfished. It's best to proceed with caution in this situation.

Wild-caught sea scallops from the North Atlantic are questionable because the fleets in this area use dredges (heavy frames and nets dragged along the sea floor) that can cause serious damage to the seabed and its ecosystem. Populations in the North Atlantic were suffering until recently, but an experimental ban on fishing has resulted in a stock recovery.

Wild-caught sea scallops from the mid-Atlantic are not a sustainable option. Not only do these fisheries depend on dredging, but populations are currently being overfished.

SIZE	TYPE	SOURCE		
Bay scallops				
Sea scallops	**Wild**	Asia	North Atlantic	**Mid-Atlantic**
	Farmed	Bottom-farmed	**Suspension farmed**	

Mercury risk: **Low**

SEA BASS / *SUZUKI*

Suzuki is a classic sushi option that is lauded in Japan but somewhat uncommon in the United States. It can be found in upscale establishments, but it cannot be considered a staple of the U.S. sushi industry.

While English speakers use the term "sea bass" to refer to many different types of fish, the word *suzuki* actually has a very precise definition—it refers to the highly sought-after Japanese sea bass, *Lateolabrax japonicus*. From time to time, one might see the term translated as "sea perch."

Some *suzuki* is taken from wild stocks, and some is raised in farms. Fishery locations range from inshore reefs off southern Japan to the northern beaches of Australia; the farms are mainly in Japan and China.

Not much is known about the strengths of various *suzuki* stocks. The Japanese sea bass matures quickly and spawns in large numbers, which would suggest an innate resilience to fishing pressure. It is interesting to note, however, that the Japanese sea bass is born male and metamorphoses into a female around age two or three. Fish exhibiting this kind of behavior are particularly vulnerable to fishing operations that target specimens of a certain size or age.

Suzuki farms also give us cause for pause. Historically, many of these farms have depended on "trash fish"—small fish from unmanaged fisheries in local waters—for feed. Luckily, it seems like a relatively small amount of feed is needed for suzuki production.

For *suzuki* lovers, there is a good alternative to Japanese sea bass. A number of farms in the United States are raising hybridized striped bass (*Morone saxatilis* crossed with *Morone chrysops*), both in ponds and in closed containment tanks. Rearing these fish requires relatively low levels of marine resources compared to what is needed to farm other species, such as Atlantic salmon or bluefin tuna. Moreover,

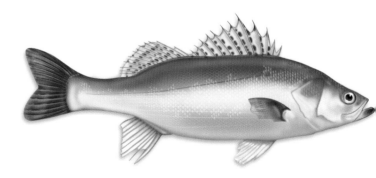

these hybrids pose no serious threat to local environments in terms of escapees or disease transfer; the tank-raised fish are an especially good choice.

There are other types of "sea bass" that find their way into U.S. sushi restaurants as well. In summary, the conscientious sushi eater's priorities should be as follows:

U.S. farm-raised hybridized striped bass is an excellent choice. They don't require a great deal of fish meal and do not endanger local ecosystems or surrounding fish populations.

Wild *suzuki* from Asia is potentially a decent option, but there are concerns. It is difficult to assess fishery health due to a general lack of science and records, especially in the fish's southern habitats. While the innate qualities of *L. japonicus* likely provide some protection from fishing pressure, it's probably better to choose the U.S. farmed product until more is known about the Asian fisheries.

Farmed *suzuki* from Asia is not well understood. It seems that most of the fish are raised in hatcheries and thus are not directly taken from wild stocks. However, little is known about the interchange between the farms and their surrounding environment.

SOURCE	TYPE	
United States		
Other sources	Farmed	Wild

Farmed striped bass mercury risk: **Low**
Japanese sea bass mercury risk: **Unknown**

SEA EEL / ANAGO

There are two types of eel that one might encounter at a U.S. sushi bar. The first, *unagi,* is the more common option and is discussed in the entry on freshwater eel. The other, *anago,* is less common, but recognition among American sushi patrons is growing.

Anago is a general term for any marine eel that does not migrate from freshwater to the sea or vice versa. Usually anago is used to mean *Conger miyaster,* the white-spotted conger, which is found in the seas around Japan. The specific term for this animal is ma-anago, or "true sea eel." In practice, however, anago refers to any type of marine eel, and the term is often translated as "conger eel" on sushi menus regardless of the actual species in question.

It should be mentioned that this same term may also be used erroneously in some sushi establishments to refer to *Muraenesox cinereus,* the daggertooth pike conger, which is of a different family. The proper Japanese term for *M. cinereus* is *hamo.*

Little is known about *anago* stocks and the environmental impact of anago fisheries. In the United States, sea eels are usually taken incidentally by fleets targeting other types of fish. Japan has a number of sea eel fisheries, some of which employ basket traps and target *Conger miyaster* in particular, but almost nothing is known about the strength of of these populations.

One of the largest problems with *anago*'s cousin, the freshwater eel, is the dubious management policies used by many Asian eel farms.

Without adequate protection measures, these farms can disseminate disease and pollution as well as interfere with local eel populations. There are also some *anago* farms in Japan, but this is a relatively new industry. Not enough is known about *anago* farming to determine whether or not farmed conger eel faces similar obstacles to those challenging the *unagi* industry.

At this point, *anago* is probably a better choice than unagi, but far too little is known about *anago* to make a solid recommendation one way or the other. Consequently, precaution is the watchword to avoid damaging stocks before we understand them better. Limit your eel consumption as much as possible, but if it's a special occasion and you must have one or the other, have *anago*.

SOURCE

Farmed

Wild

Mercury risk: Low

SEA URCHIN / UNI

雲
云
丹

Strongylocentrotus spp.

The difference between a delicacy and mere food is more than taste or texture; it includes the odd and sometimes baffling source of the dish. In no case is this truer than with the humble sea urchin. A homely little cluster of spines, this ornery creature is dreaded by waders and barefoot beachcombers alike. But the gonads of the sea urchin, slurped down with rice and maybe a bit of *nihonshu*, are one of the most sensual of sushi delights: *uni*.

It has become commonplace for sushi devotees to round out their meals with the tonguelike sexual organs of these spiky animals, and *uni* is a common favorite in both Japanese and U.S. sushi establishments. This popularity makes it all the more important to differentiate between the many different *uni* fisheries in the world. While some deserve our support, others should be avoided at all costs.

In the United States we generally consume red and green sea urchins, both of which are members of the *Strongylocentrotus* genus. Green sea urchins (*S. droebachiensis*), found on both the Atlantic and Pacific coasts, show a preference for colder climes—Washington State to Alaska in the west, New Jersey to the Arctic Ocean in the east. Red sea urchins (*S. franciscanus*), which can range from the color of old brick to a deep majestic purple, are found only in the Pacific. Their populations stretch from Baja California to Alaska. Most of our red and green uni is either domestic product or imported from Canada, but we also import uni from Japan. Almost all fisheries hand-gather urchins using divers, so bycatch (unintended species and juveniles that are caught and discarded) is very low.

UNI / SEA URCHIN

The main issues facing *uni* fisheries are relatively simple—how many sea urchins are left, and are there rules in place to protect them?

Red and green sea urchins from British Columbia are a good way to satisfy your *uni* craving. Strong populations of both species are overseen by proactive management and are protected by stiff quotas.

Green sea urchins from New Brunswick are also a positive choice. Populations appear relatively healthy, and management is in place to keep them that way.

Red sea urchins from California are a less defensible choice. The management regime, which does not use quotas and has no effective enforcement measures, has not been able to prevent significant declines in populations.

Uni from Japan is still very much an open question. Little is known about the status of Japanese sea urchin stocks, and at this point it's probably better to pass on Japanese sea urchin in favor of Canadian.

Green sea urchins from Maine must be avoided. Stock strengths are at approximately ten percent of what they once were and are continuing to decline. We must ease the pressure on this fishery to allow populations to recover.

SOURCE
British Columbia
New Brunswick
California
Maine
Japan

Mercury risk: Low

SHRIMP / *EBI*

Shrimp is the most popular seafood item in the United States. Over the past two decades, it has transformed from a relatively expensive delicacy into a staple of the American diet. Shrimp has recently surpassed such long-standing icons as salmon and canned tuna in popularity, and it is now the basis of a multibillion-dollar global industry.

Ebi is an ambiguous term at the sushi bar that can refer to either shrimp or prawns. The classic way to serve *ebi* is cooked as nigiri. *Ama ebi*, on the other hand, is usually served raw. In the United States, shrimp is generally used for *nigiri*, while spot prawns are used for *ama ebi*. This is not always the case, of course, but the delineation serves as a useful guideline when trying to determine what is on one's plate.

Our increasing consumption of shrimp has prompted a great deal of publicity about various related health and environmental impacts. Americans devour farmed and wild shrimp in great quantities, both of which can be found at the sushi bar. The various fisheries present different pros and cons, but the shrimp puzzle is not as indecipherable as it may seem.

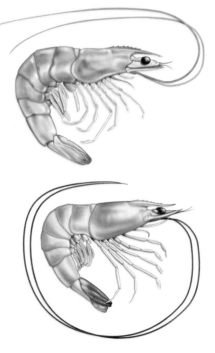

Panaeus vannemei, the Pacific white shrimp, is one of the most commonly farmed shrimps in the world.

A wild white shrimp from the Gulf of Mexico

Wild shrimp are caught in most of the planet's oceans and support dozens of shrimp industries around the world. There are typically three major problems in wild shrimp fisheries:

Bycatch: Many shrimp fisheries unintentionally catch unacceptably large numbers of other animals. Some shrimpers have been known to discard more than ten pounds of unwanted sea life for every pound of shrimp they keep.

Habitat destruction: Shrimp are often bottom-trawled—caught in large nets dragged along the sea bottom. In addition to the bycatch issue, this bottom trawling can severely damage the seabed and disturb or kill bottom-dwelling animals, corals, and aquatic plants.

Stock depletion: Some shrimp populations have simply been over-fished. Shrimp are generally resilient to this kind of pressure due to their rapid growth rate and prolific nature, but resilience does not equal immunity.

Farmed shrimp are cultivated in ponds, marshes, and lagoons all over the world. Here's a quick rundown of the problems facing the farmed shrimp industry:

Habitat destruction: The traditional shrimp farm is created by clear-cutting mangrove plants and erecting embankments to cordon off the area. Millions of acres of mangroves have been cut down to make room for shrimp farms. This approach is less common today than it was a decade ago, but mangrove depletion remains a major problem.

Feed: Shrimp demand a great deal of protein. While they are able to eat just about anything, the historic solution has been to grind up vast quantities of fish and dump it into the shrimp pond. Fortunately the shrimp industry has evolved, developing many types of manufactured feed. Unfortunately the "reduction fisheries" that supply the basis

Farmed shrimp, nigiri style

for this feed often have little or no management in place. A new feed based on algae is attempting to penetrate the market, but until it becomes commercially viable the feed issue will continue to thwart the industry's progress toward sustainability.

Pollution: The wastewater from certain shrimp ponds can be highly toxic, especially if many generations of shrimp have been raised at that location. Tropical storms can breach the barriers surrounding the ponds, allowing vast amounts of contaminated water to pollute the nearby sea. This has been known to have devastating effects on the local bottom-dwelling habitat.

So how does one select sustainably farmed shrimp?

U.S. farmed shrimp and freshwater prawns are rapidly evolving industries that have shown true progress over the past few years. They are a much better option than most Asian imports—more environmental regulations are in place, higher levels of accountability and transparency prevail, and in general the product is cleaner.

Imported farmed shrimp, such as tiger prawns, should be avoided. There are simply too many problems and potential dangers associated with this industry for it to merit our patronage. Some farms do outperform others, but there is not yet a strong certification system in place.

And for wild products:

British Columbia spot prawns, known to be well-managed and caught with environmentally responsible traps, are an excellent option. They are commonly used in *ama ebi* dishes in the United States.

Oregon pink shrimp are also caught and managed in a thoughtful and progressive manner. Such shrimp are a sustainable option and should be supported, but this fishery produces a smaller product (salad shrimp) that is not often used in sushi bars.

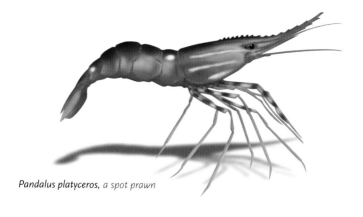

Pandalus platyceros, a spot prawn

British Columbian spot prawns as ama ebi

U.S. spot prawns are also a better choice than imported Asian products. However, since little is known about the population status of this fishery, caution is suggested.

U.S. wild shrimp from the Pacific coast, Gulf of Mexico, and mid-Atlantic Ocean is an acceptable choice with better management practices than most imported alternatives. Unfortunately, bycatch remains a problem in many U.S. shrimp fisheries. The **New England wild shrimp** fishery is known to be particularly destructive to the local habitat.

Wild Asian shrimp fisheries are often poorly managed, and little is known about the status of their various stocks. It's better to select shrimp from a better-understood and better-managed fishery.

TYPE	SOURCE		
Farmed shrimp	US	Imported	
Wild shrimp	Asia	New England	Other U.S. sources
Spot prawns	British Columbia	United States	

Mercury risk: Low

SNAPPER / *TAI*

Tai is a fish of many faces. The English equivalent of the word is usually considered to be "snapper," an equally ambiguous term that means very little. Just about anything can be called a snapper, but usually it refers to some type of a long-living fish that grows slowly and lives in rocky areas. These fish are also tagged with other meaningless monikers like "sea bream" and "sea perch." None of this makes it any easier to choose sustainable *tai*.

In Japan the preferred option is generally *Pagrus major*. This fish is in high demand and is known by a number of English names, most commonly red sea bream and Japanese sea perch. The technical Japanese term for this fish is *madai,* or "true *tai.*"

Madai is extremely popular in Japan, and it is traditionally served at celebrations and festive occasions. This cultural significance, coupled with North Americans' historic indifference to the fish, has forestalled any major exports of the product to the United States. This situation is beginning to change, however. *Madai* aquaculture is a major industry in Japan, Taiwan, and China, and some of these farms are now selling their product to the Western market. Even so, *madai* is not yet readily available in North America, so more accessible alternatives are often served in its place.

Madai prepared as sashimi

TAI / SNAPPER

Sushi bars in the southern United States and along parts of the East Coast often use *Pagrus pagrus*, the red porgy, as *tai*. Red porgy is caught along the Atlantic coast of Florida and in the Gulf of Mexico. Historically the Atlantic fishery has been the more productive of the two, but

stocks fell sharply during the late twentieth century. It was not until after fish populations had been significantly depleted that any management protocols were put in place.

Pagrus major, the Japanese "*king of fish,*" a.k.a. **madai**

As red porgy landings declined in the Atlantic fishery, they began to increase in the Gulf of Mexico. Currently the majority of red porgy consumed in the United States is caught in this region. Unfortunately, there have been no stock assessments conducted on Gulf of Mexico red porgy populations, and beyond state waters, there is no management in place.

If the *tai* at your local sushi restaurant isn't Japanese sea perch or red porgy, it might be *Lutjanus campechanus*, the ubiquitous red snapper. This popular fish is also caught primarily in the Gulf of Mexico, and like the red porgy it is potentially in serious trouble. Stocks are known to be overfished, but they are still being exploited at levels beyond what the population can support.

SNAPPER / *TAI* *continued*

There is also a significant amount of red snapper imported into the United States, mainly from Latin America. Little in known about the status of these stocks, but it is possible that they are facing problems similar to those of domestic red snapper.

Vermillion snapper is also caught in the Gulf of Mexico. Like red snapper, vermillion snapper is overfished, and although there is management in place, populations continue to decline.

Finally, the newest addition to the lineup is *Pagrus auratus*, often known as New Zealand *tai* snapper, or *kodai*. There are several *tai* snapper fisheries in the waters around New Zealand. Known as *tamure* among the Maori, the native people of New Zealand, this fish has long been of great importance to New Zealanders, but it has only recently gained a following in the United States. The current situation is somewhat chaotic: A number of the fisheries are overfished and poorly managed, while others boast healthy populations and strong management.

Here's how *tai* plays out at the sushi bar:

Farmed *madai* imported from Asia is potentially a better choice than domestic wild alternatives. That being said, it can be difficult to locate. Moreover, not enough is known about farm management or environmental impacts to justify an unalloyed recommendation.

Wild red porgy from the Atlantic is not a perfect choice, but there is management in place now, and stocks seem to be recovering.

Wild red porgy from the Gulf of Mexico is potentially an unsustainable choice, but not enough is known to say for certain. Still, until more

Pagrus auratus, *New Zealand tai snapper,*
a.k.a. **kodai**

research is done on stock strength and strong management protocols are imposed, this fishery will continue to be a free-for-all.

Red snapper from the Gulf of Mexico is dangerous as well. The stocks are weak and only growing weaker as overzealous fishing pressure continues.

Vermillion snapper from the Gulf of Mexico is also a risky selection. Until populations stop declining and begin to rebuild, it is best to select a more sustainable option.

Other snappers from the Gulf of Mexico are more difficult to assess. Some chefs may use yellowtail, gray, lane, or mutton snappers as *tai*. Yellowtail snapper populations look healthy, but there isn't enough information available to be sure. Even less is known about the other snapper populations, so order these species with some caution.

Red snapper imported from Latin America poses a difficult problem. Not enough is known about it to justify a red ranking. However, many believe that Latin American stocks may be suffering like those in the Gulf of Mexico. It's best to be cautious.

New Zealand *tai* snapper is not perfect, but management does exist, and the stock status is fairly well understood. This is potentially a better choice then most of the other common options.

Perhaps the most difficult aspect of enjoying *tai* is the general lack of knowledge as to what species is actually being served. As a general rule, consider bypassing *tai* for other options—U.S. farmed striped bass and barramundi are both excellent alternatives.

SOURCE	SPECIES			
Japan	Madai			
New Zealand				
U.S. Atlantic				
Gulf of Mexico	Red porgy	**Red snapper**	**Vermillion snapper**	Other snapper
Other sources				

Mercury risk: Low

SPANISH MACKEREL / *SAWARA*

Scomberomorus spp.

The Spanish mackerel is a sleek oceanic schooling fish that boasts a smattering of orange spots along its flanks. There are many different species of Spanish mackerel, but the term *sawara* is usually used for *Scomberomorus niphonius*, the Japanese Spanish mackerel. This fish is very popular in Japan but has only recently achieved any real following in North America. U.S. sushi bars will often offer related *Scomberomorus* species from the Atlantic Ocean or the Gulf of Mexico as *sawara*.

If your sushi restaurant offers Spanish mackerel as *aji*, the term is being mistranslated. *Aji* is specifically horse mackerel, a related but distinctly different genus of fish. The *aji* section in this book discusses the issues related to the horse mackerel. As for Spanish mackerel, it grows rapidly and reaches sexual maturity relatively early. These characteristics help to protect the species from fishing pressure.

There is a large Spanish mackerel fishery in the Gulf of Mexico that is well-managed and based on strong stocks. The populations are neither depleted nor currently being overfished. The majority of the domestic fleet targets Spanish mackerel with gill nets, which have little

impact on the surrounding habitat. There is, however, some bycatch or unintended catch of marine mammals in the fishery, a concern which should be kept in mind when ordering this fish.

The term *sawara* can also refer to *Scomberomorus carvalla,* the king mackerel. While both this fish and its Spanish cousin may contain elevated levels of mercury, king mackerel can be a serious threat. It is a large fish that exists at the top of the food chain and has been found to contain exceptionally high quantities of mercury. Stocks are strong, and the king mackerel fishery is generally well-managed, but numerous scientific sources have concluded that king mackerel is unsafe and should be avoided, especially by small children and pregnant women.

In terms of sustainability, *sawara* is a good choice at the sushi bar. Both Spanish mackerel and king mackerel have strong stocks and good management in place—just be attentive to the mercury issue, especially if the *sawara* in question turns out to be royalty.

SPECIES	SOURCE		
Aji (horse mackerel)	**Domestic**	Imported	
Saba (Atlantic mackerel)	**Domestic**	**Marine Stewardship Council-certified imported**	Other imported
Sawara (Spanish or king mackerel)			

Mercury risk: **High**

SQUID / IKA

In the last decade or two, squid has gone from a standard item in bait shops to a staple in restaurants across the United States. Although long hailed as a culinary delicacy in Europe, Asia, and elsewhere, these many-tentacled cephalopods tended to make American appetites shrivel until relatively recently. Today, squid is a daily menu item in white-tablecloth establishments from San Diego to New York.

As with many other fisheries, this recent increase in popularity has put new boats in the water and increased pressure on squid populations. Squid trawlers emit an eerie glow at night as they ply the coasts of central California and the Eastern Seaboard, dragging their nets through the water. The lights atop the ships serve to lure the squid to the surface.

Oftentimes the "squid" available in sushi restaurants isn't squid at all—it's cuttlefish, a related but distinctly different species. Most of these cuttlefish come from the waters around Vietnam. Unfortunately, very little is known about this fishery, so it is difficult to make an informed recommendation. As always, it is best to use moderation when dealing with the unknown.

Most of the true squid served in U.S. sushi restaurants is flown in from Japan, but occasionally domestic product is used, usually in appetizers.

There are three main types of squid available in the United States—long-fin, short-fin, and Humboldt or jumbo squid. Long-fin and short-fin squid are small in size and are caught in the Atlantic Ocean. The much larger Humboldt squid, which can easily exceed three feet in length, are found along the U.S. West Coast or the Gulf of California in Mexico. Unfortunately for the consumer, it is nearly impossible to tell these species apart when they are prepared as your dinner.

Loligo pealei, the long-fin squid

Squid grow quickly, reach maturity within a single year, and reproduce in large numbers. These characteristics help to keep populations strong even when they are heavily fished. These animals also generally school over sandy habitats, which are more resilient to the effects of trawling than rocky areas. However, no sea creature is immune to depletion and devastation if exploited too heavily—squid may have a number of factors on their side, but there is still little known about actual population dynamics.

If possible, try to aim for long-fin squid from the East Coast; more is known about this fishery than about the others, and it seems to be fairly well-managed with strong populations.

In general, squid is a good alternative to less sustainable options at the sushi bar.

SPECIES	SOURCE		
Long-fin squid	**U.S. Atlantic**	Other U.S. sources	Imported
Short-fin squid			
Humboldt squid			
Other squid species			
Cuttlefish			

Mercury risk: Low

SURF CLAMS / *HOKKIGAI*

Mactromeris polynyma, a.k.a. Spisula polynyma

With its triangular shape and swollen red foot, *hokkigai* is one of the most easily identifiable options at the sushi bar. Although native to North America, it has become a delicacy in Japan and is common in sushi restaurants on both sides of the Pacific.

Known both as the arctic surf clam and Stimpson's surf clam, *hokkigai* is a long-lived burrowing bivalve usually caught in the waters off Quebec, Nova Scotia, and Newfoundland. Although there is also a fishery in Alaska, most *hokkigai* in the sushi market comes from Eastern Canada.

Surf clams don't reach sexual maturity until five to eight years of age and can live for many decades in their natural habitat. Although they have been heavily targeted by Canadian clammers, there is very little information on the strength of surf clam stocks. This is a concern, but the larger issue is the way these clams are harvested.

Surf clams are caught using a hydraulic dredge— a portable high-powered vacuum that literally tears the ocean floor apart in search of its quarry. This disturbance may cause severe problems for other life forms in the area. In fact, tests on clam beds exploited in this manner have revealed few signs of recovery, even after as long as three years. Any number of cohabiting species, such as groundfish, other invertebrates, or aquatic plants, can be severely impacted by dredging. At best they are forced to relocate, but many creatures are injured or killed in the process.

Spisula polynyma

HOKKIGAI / SURF CLAMS

Unfortunately, this method of gathering sea life is not restricted to *hokkigai*. It is employed in numerous wild bivalve fisheries. While there may be a few small hokkigai fisheries that don't use hydraulic dredges, it's best to seek out farm-raised alternatives to these wild bivalves.

In some sushi bars, particularly on the East Coast of the United States, it may be possible to find local Atlantic surf clams as hokkigai. While this is extremely rare, it is likely a better option than Canadian product as more is known about the sustainability of the domestic fishery. Still, these clams are hydraulically dredged in a manner similar to their arctic relatives to the north, which is far from an optimal collection process.

There are better options than *hokkigai* at the sushi bar. Farmed abalone, scallops, and geoduck are all delicious and taken in a manner far less destructive to their environments.

SPECIES

Atlantic surf clam

Arctic surf clam

Mercury risk: Low

WHITE TREVALLY / *SHIMAAJI*

Pseudocaranx dentex

Lamentably, it's not easy to find *shimaaji* in the United States. The sweet delicate flesh of the white trevally, usually labeled on menus as "striped jack," is often described as a cross between *aji* and *hamachi*—a truly succulent combination. If you haven't tried it, it's something to experience.

But to try it, first you have to find it. And in North American sushi bars, that's not easy.

There are those who say that everything happens for a reason. If that's the case, then one might wonder: *Why is it so hard for those of us in the United States to get our hands on* shimaaji?

Well, how's this for a theory—we can't get it because if we did, we would eat it, we would like it, and we would want more. And that just might be a problem.

The challenge with white trevally is that it is an unknown. When it comes to delicious but endangered fish like the bluefin tuna, we have solid reasons to cut back. I can cite bycatch (unintended species and juveniles that are caught and discarded), mercury, population crashes, and ecosystem effects as legitimate bases to give bluefin a miss. But *shimaaji*? I can't make much of an argument because compared to many other fish, we know virtually nothing about it.

White trevally occurs throughout much of the world in temperate, subtropical, and tropical zones between the low-tide mark and the edge of

the continental shelf. It's caught incidentally in many of these areas, but the Japanese sushi industry, which consumes vast quantities of *shimaaji*, only uses fish caught in Japanese waters. So although white trevally is found off the shores of Ireland, Tasmania, North Carolina, and a dozen other places, all the pressure seems to be on the Japanese fishery. Why is that? I don't know.

The intrinsic characteristics of white trevally include a moderate growth rate, mediocre spawning capabilities, and a potential maximum age of over forty years. This doesn't sound ideal from an environmental standpoint; then again, there is a pronounced paucity of science and stock assessment data. So how does it all translate to sustainability? I'm not sure.

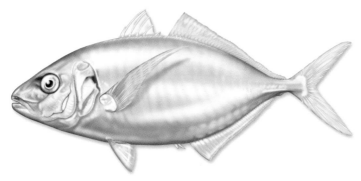

Deep in the Pacific Ocean about five hundred miles south of Tokyo there is a small island known as Chichijima. Some sources say that on this tiny island, fish farmers collect the eggs of white trevally and raise the fish in captivity to meet the consumer demand. Is white trevally farmed in such a manner a better option than the wild product? I have no idea.

There is, however, one thing that I am certain of: *Shimaaji* is delicious. It is regarded as a luxury fish in Japan, and only a tiny fraction of the catch is exported. And however dangerous it may be for a fish to mature late, or to grow at a snail's pace, or to reproduce in small numbers—nothing is quite as dangerous as tasting good.

So be careful with *shimaaji*. If you have a chance, give it a try, but think twice before heading back for more.

SOURCE	TYPE	
Japan	Farmed	Wild
Other sources		

Mercury risk: Unknown

GROCERY STORE SUSHI

Raw fish and *wasabi* aren't just for restaurants anymore. Many Americans now get their sushi fixes at grocery stores. This is not to be ignored. Grocery store sushi, while convenient and often inexpensive, brings with it a host of problems.

We've already discussed the fish that one finds inside these boxes (most commonly farmed salmon, longlined tuna, and farmed freshwater eel: bad, bad, and bad), but at the grocery store, the issues go deeper. It's not just the sushi that's a concern—it's the packaging.

The lid: The clear top of your average grocery store sushi container is made from the easy-to-find but difficult-to-pronounce polyethylene terephthalate—PET, or number 1 plastic. It is identifiable by its logo, a "1" encircled by three chasing arrows in a triangle. PET is one of the most common packaging plastics in use today. PET plastics are recyclable, but more common PET plastic items, like water bottles, are recycled separately from sushi lids. Because of this, these lids incur added operational costs for the plants, so they are usually ignored by brokers. You may drop your lid into the recycling bin, but if no broker purchases it, it ends up getting mixed back in with the nonrecyclable trash. While many disposable products made from PET plastics are often recycled into clothing like polar fleece and

other polyester products, your sushi lid is probably going to be a sushi lid for the rest of its days. And given that PET plastic theoretically lasts for thousands of years, that's a lot of days.

The base: The black plastic box cradling your California roll or *nigiri* special is an even bigger problem. This time the culprit is made of polystyrene—PS, or number 6 plastic, identified by a "6" in the recycling logo. Polystyrene is used for a staggering multitude of purposes due to its versatility: When gases are injected into it, it becomes Styrofoam. Polystyrene is technically recyclable, but there are very few processing facilities that are capable of doing so. It is nearly certain that even if you drop it in the recycling bin, it's still going to the landfill—or worse, into the ocean. Also somewhat troubling are the potential links

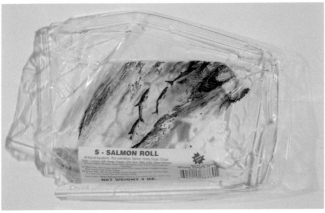

between number 6 plastic and health effects; studies suggest toxic chemicals may transfer from polystyrene containers into food through heat exchange. Yum.

The sticks: Most disposable chopsticks are made from a mixture of bamboo and rapidly growing lightweight wood, such as poplar or balsa. In China alone in 2006, over fifty billion pairs of chopsticks were produced, used once, and thrown away. Ironically, it has been the disposable chopstick industry that has prompted much of the environmental awareness that is growing in Chinese culture. Many people now bring their own chopsticks with them when they dine out—a small but important step toward resource conservation.

We need to demand more than just sustainable fish from our grocery stores—responsible sushi should be presented in a responsible manner. Our ability to effectively recycle the materials we use needs to keep pace with our manufacturing output. There are also biodegradable alternatives to PET plastic and polystyrene that could serve the same purpose. This may be a bit more expensive in the short-run, but these kinds of changes will help us transition to a cleaner, healthier world.

AFTERWORD: *Taking It Further*

In our world of growing populations and shrinking resources, changing the dining habits of a few individuals isn't going to end starvation or bring about world peace. **Sustainable Sushi** isn't trying to fool anyone into believing that. Rather, the point of this book is to help you start thinking about sustainability in all aspects of life.

That being said, don't underestimate the importance of your choices at the sushi bar. When we start asking questions and eschewing options like bluefin tuna in favor of more sustainable choices, we send a message that we care about the impact of the food we eat. Our actions demonstrate that we think about how our food is raised or captured, and our concern proves that the values behind our food are more important than its flavor.

Those individuals willing to think this way, to pass on a delicacy or forgo an old favorite because they believe in a sustainable lifestyle; they are the future of this planet.

So, what's the next step? How can we move beyond *Sustainable Sushi*?

First of all, we must realize that we need to eat less fish in general. If we are to resuscitate our ailing oceans, we must ease the pressure on fish populations. With that idea in mind, I'd like to make a suggestion: One of these days when you find yourself salivating for sushi, consider making it at home. "Domestic" sushi not only satisfies your cravings, it allows you to experiment with some alternatives to fish.

I can guess what some of you are thinking—vegetarian sushi doesn't have the same appeal, or strike the same chord, that your favorite piece of fish does. But perhaps that's because most sushi restaurants only serve one or two (usually boring) vegetarian options.

You're probably already familiar with the usual suspects of the vegetarian and vegan sushi ensemble. Staples like cucumber, burdock, avocado, and daikon are common in sushi bars all over the United States. But let's face it: *kappa maki* and its confederates simply get old after a while.

So in an effort to revitalize your interest in vegetarian and vegan options, here are a few delicious alternatives to fish that you can use when rolling sushi at home.

Sweet potatoes or yams: I'm not kidding. Boil a sweet potato, mash it up with sesame oil and maybe a little maple syrup, let it cool, and spread it in the center of a roll. You'll be floored.

Mushrooms: Tasty fungi can bring some zest and bulk to a veggie roll. Slice up some shiitakes and marinate them in a sauce of your own concoction—red peppers and rice vinegar, garlic brine, or herbs and balsamic vinegar are just a few delectable options.

Green apple: A crisp, thinly sliced Granny Smith apple can bring a tart zing and a touch of sweetness to sushi, not to mention a crunchy texture. This ingredient goes well with macadamia nuts.

Strawberries: One of my favorites. Get some ripe strawberries, slice them thinly, and layer them in the roll. They bring a burst of ripe sweetness to the dish.

Japanese eggplant: Known as *nasu,* eggplant is a traditional Japanese ingredient in numerous dishes. It can be prepared in many different ways; for example, it's delicious sliced, grilled, and marinated for a few minutes in soy, *mirin,* and ginger, and can bring spice and depth to a sushi roll.

Mango: Another personal favorite. I tend to use mango in sushi even when I'm not making vegan dishes. It combines perfectly with sticky rice and brings a soft richness to the roll that is surprisingly reminiscent of *hamachi.*

Almond butter: Now we're getting creative. I learned to use almond butter in sushi from a couple of good friends. The flavor

has an earthiness that works well to anchor more buoyant flavors, like strawberries. Don't use too much, though—this stuff is sticky.

Macadamia nuts: This treat is just starting to hit the mainstream. Crush the nuts and sprinkle them on top of a roll. These wonderful little bits of fat and protein help round out the nutritional aspects of a vegetarian sushi meal.

Vegan *wasabi* aioli: A touch of this stuff can really smooth out the texture of a roll while giving it a little kick. To make it, just add

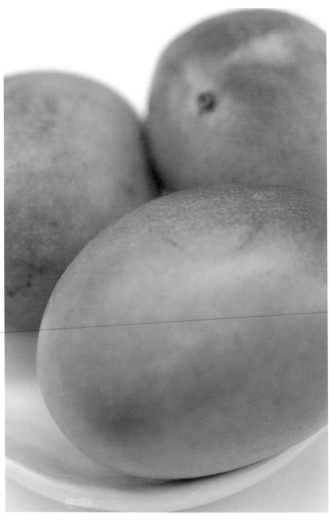

wasabi paste to mayonnaise or whatever vegan alternative you use in its place. My only caution is to be sparing, as it's rich.

Pineapple: Want a sweet, crisp dish to cleanse your palate or finish off your meal? Try a pineapple roll. Add some crushed macadamia nuts for texture and some sliced kiwi fruit for variety. If you're a fish eater, pineapple pairs fabulously with shrimp—the sustainable variety, of course.

Seasoned *aburage:* These are the tofu pouches used to make *inari.* Not long ago I started slicing them up and using them to fill *maki.* They're easy to make and a great vegan replacement for *tamago.*

When all is said and done, it's up to all of us to take responsibility for our actions. Our ecosystem is fragile, and its future is very much in our hands. So eat with your heart. Let your ethics guide your spending—you can vote with your dollars to make your voice heard. Gandhi told us to be the change that we want to see in the world; all I'm suggesting is that the sushi bar is a pretty good place to start.

ABOUT THE AUTHOR

Born in Seattle and living in San Francisco, Casson Trenor has traveled to over forty countries researching fisheries and marine resources. He holds an MA in International Environmental Policy from the prestigious Monterey Institute of International Studies and is the central character in *The Whale Warriors*, journalist Peter Heller's chronicle of the 2005 mission to end illegal whaling in the Southern Ocean.

GLOSSARY OF JAPANESE TERMS

aburage: Thinly sliced deep-fried tofu. Mainly used for wrapping *inari* and preparing *miso* soup.

aburasokomutsu: Escolar.

aji: Horse mackerel. Often erroneously translated as "Spanish mackerel" on menus.

akami: The lean side cut of a tuna.

anago: An ambiguous term for any marine eel. Usually used in reference to members of the genus *Conger*.

ankimo: The liver of the monkfish *(anko)*, which is generally steamed or smoked.

anko: Monkfish.

awabi: Abalone.

binnagamaguro: An alternate term for *shiromaguro*, the albacore tuna.

buri: Adult Japanese amberjack.

chu-toro: A somewhat fatty cut from the sides of a tuna belly.

ebi: Shrimp.

edomae: Literally, "in front of Tokyo." Refers to the style of sushi that is popular in Tokyo and the Kanto region.

gindara: Sablefish.

hagatsuo: Bonito.

hamachi: Japanese amberjack. Often mistranslated as "yellowtail" or "yellowtail amberjack."

hamo: Daggertooth pike conger. Extremely rare in North American sushi bars.

hashi: Chopsticks.

hikari mono: A term referring to fish prepared with its silvery skin still on. Some common examples are saury, halfbeak, and mackerel.

hiramasa: Yellowtail amberjack.

hirame: An ambiguous term for flatfish.

hokkigai: Surf clam.

honmaguro: Bluefin tuna. Effectively synonymous with *kuromaguro.*

hotate: Scallop. Also written as *hotategai.*

ika: Squid.

inari: formally *inarizushi;* an *aburage* pouch stuffed with vinegared rice and other ingredients.

iwana: Char.

iwashi: Sardine.

kaki: Oyster.

kani: Crab.

kanikama: Imitation crab.

kanpachi: Greater amberjack. Also used to refer to almaco jack in certain farming operations.

kappa maki: A simple cucumber roll. The word *kappa* actually means "water goblin" in Japanese; the name of the dish derives from Japanese mythology.

karafuto-shishamo: Capelin.

karei: Flounder, fluke, or sole.

katsuo: Skipjack tuna. Also used to refer to bonito, which is technically *hagatsuo.*

katsuobushi: Dried fish flakes made from skipjack tuna or bonito. Used for flavoring and garnish.

kihada: Yellowfin tuna.

kohada: Gizzard shad at approximately four inches in length. Follows the *shinko* stage and precedes the *nakazumi* stage. This is the most common size of gizzard shad in U.S. sushi bars.

konoshiro: Gizzard shad at a length of seven inches or greater. Follows the *nakazumi* stage. Not generally used in sushi.

kuromaguro: Bluefin tuna. Effectively synonymous with *honmaguro.*

ma-: A Japanese prefix meaning "true." Often used to indicate specific species of fish, generally of high regard. Examples include *madai* (red sea bream, literally "true snapper"), *maanago* (the white-spotted conger eel), and *madako* (the common octopus).

maguro: Tuna.

maki: formally *makizushi;* a sushi "roll" made using a bamboo mat. Classic combinations involve a layer of fish or vegetables surrounded by vinegared rice and wrapped in *nori.*

masago: Capelin roe (eggs).

mebachi: Bigeye tuna.

mirin: A sweet Japanese cooking wine made from rice.

mirugai: Geoduck. Often translated as "giant clam" on menus.

nakazuki: Gizzard shad at approximately six inches in length. Follows the *kohada* stage and precedes the *konoshiro* stage.

nasu: Japanese eggplant.

nigiri: formally *nigirizushi;* literally "hand-molded." Refers to an ovoid clump of vinegared sushi rice topped with another ingredient, usually fish. Often wrapped with a thin strip of *nori.*

nihonshu: Japanese rice wine, commonly included in the blanket term *sake.*

nori: A type of seaweed used frequently in sushi dishes.

ohyo: Halibut.

o-toro: A fatty cut from the center of a tuna belly.

saba: Mackerel.

sake: Salmon. Pronounced both "sa-kay" and "sha-kay" depending on location.

sake: The Japanese word for alcohol or alcoholic beverages. Used in the United States to refer to Japanese rice wine *(nihonshu).*

sanma: Pacific saury.

sashimi: Raw fish or meat in any form. Often refers to raw fish served in slices and accompanied by soy sauce, pickled ginger, and *wasabi.*

sawara: Spanish mackerel. This term can also refer to king mackerel.

sayori: Halfbeak.

sazae: Conch.

shimaaji: White trevally. Often known as "striped jack."

shinko: Gizzard shad at approximately two inches in length. Precedes the *kohada* stage. This is the most expensive size of gizzard shad.

shiromaguro: A menu term for albacore tuna.

sunomono: Vinegared salad. Generally contains cucumbers and may also incorporate crab, octopus or other seafood.

surimi: A mixture of fish, sugar, and starch that is used to make various processed fish products, such as imitation crab.

suzuki: Japanese sea bass. In the United States the term may refer to other fish.

tai: An ambiguous term for snapper. Often refers to members of the genus *Pagrus,* but this is not always the case.

tako: A general term for octopus.

tamago: The Japanese word for "egg." In sushi bars this word is used in reference to a sweet omelet that is prepared especially for use in sushi.

tobiko: The eggs of the flying fish.

tobiuo: Flying fish.

toro: An ambiguous term referring to a fatty cut from the belly of a fish, generally tuna.

unagi: Freshwater eel.

uni: Sea urchin.

uzura no tamago: Quail egg.

INDEX